Selected Po

DENISE RILEY is a critically acclaimed writer of both
philosophy and poetry. She is currently Professor of the
History of Ideas and of Poetry at UEA. Her visiting positions
have included A. D. White Professor at Cornell University
in the US, Writer in Residence at the Tate Gallery in London,
and Visiting Fellow at Birkbeck College in the University of
London. She has taught philosophy, social and political
history, art history and poetry. She is the author of
Say Something Back and lives in London.

ALSO BY DENISE RILEY

Poetry

Marxism for Infants

No Fee, with Wendy Mulford

Dry Air

Stair Spirit

Mop Mop Georgette

Say Something Back

Prose

War in the Nursery:
Theories of the Child and Mother

'Am I That Name?':
Feminism and the Category of Women in History

The Words of Selves:
Identification, Solidarity, Irony

Impersonal Passion: Language as Affect

Time Lived, Without Its Flow

Denise Riley

Selected Poems
1976–2016

PICADOR

First published 2019 by Picador
an imprint of Pan Macmillan
20 New Wharf Road, London N1 9RR
Associated companies throughout the world
www.panmacmillan.com

ISBN 978-1-5290-1712-0

1 3 5 7 9 8 6 4 2

A CIP catalogue record for this book is available from the British Library.

Printed and bound by CPI Group (UK) Ltd, Croydon, CR0 4YY

Visit **www.picador.com** to read more about all our books
and to buy them. You will also find features, author interviews and
news of any author events, and you can sign up for e-newsletters
so that you're always first to hear about our new releases.

Contents

[v]

[vi]

From MARXISM FOR INFANTS
(1977)

A note on sex and 'the reclaiming of language'

The 'Savage' is flying back home from the New Country
in native-style dress with a baggage of sensibility
to gaze on the ancestral plains with the myths thought up
and dreamed in her kitchens as guides

                She will be discovered
as meaning is flocking densely around the words seeking a way
any way in between the gaps, like a fertilisation

                The work is
e.g. to write 'she' and for that to be a statement
of fact only, and not a strong image
of everything which is not-you, which sees you

The new land is colonised, though its prospects are empty

The 'Savage' weeps as landing at the airport
she is asked to buy wood carvings, which represent herself

Making a Liberty Belle

my exercise book of twenty
years ago says neatly, I guess
copied out of an Annual:
'to make a Liberty Belle
White Ballet
Skirt with a
Layer of Blue Net
Dotted with
Silver Stars.
Back and Front
Panels Red White
Striped Cotton.
Tie Bandolier of White Stuff
Over One Shoulder
and under opposite, write
word "LIBERTY" in Indian
Ink.   Cut headdress from
Gold or painted paper
Cornet of same
with screw
of orangey-red paper inside
to represent the Flame'

she's imagining her wife & how will she live her? when
the wife goes off to endless meetings in the rain
she'll say aah I admire her spirit, bravo la petite
& when her belly swells into an improbable curve
the she-husband will think Yes, it was me who caused that,
and more generously, Biology, you are wonderful

postcard: 'I live in silence here
a wet winter   the baby's well
I give her bears' names   Ursula
Mischa   Pola   Living alone makes
anyone crazy, especially with children'

I live in silence here

the tongue as a swan's neck
full and heavy in the mouth

speech as a sexed thing

the speaking limb is stilled

She has ingested her wife
she has re-inhabited her own wrists
she is squatting in her own temples, the
fall of light on hair or any decoration
is re-possessed.   'She' is I.

There's nothing for it   Your 'father' and I
Biologically, a lack   The child tries manfully
He calls it special seed but he gets confused at school

An unselfconscious wife is raised high as a flag over the
                                    playground and burns up

I heard the water freezing in a thousand launderettes
with a dense white shudder
I heard the roar of a thousand vacuum cleaners
stammer away into uncarpeted silence

today it is all grandiose domestic visions truly

in St Petersburg now Leningrad we have communal kitchens
the cooking is dreadful but we get to meet our friends

An infant

who lives in 'feminism' like a warm square
who composes 'pushes hair back wearily' on a bicycle
who has always been older than twenty-eight and is half-killed
                                                    in oldness
who doubts daily and is silly for something or other

who comes in the shut house where she is

whose face is floating in its still sleep skin
whose face is features under clear water
whose days come bursting purely to her surface

who is watched asleep in a hawk's heart
who is hovered over in a passion
who is new enough not to mind that
who is perfectly right enough to be generous

whose fingers have a fresh will
whose face is all its future

it's November, child, and time goes
in little bursts   a warm room
clean and squeaky as an orange pip
in a wet landscape

You have a family?   It is impermissible.

There is only myself   complete and arched
like a rainbow or an old tree
with gracious arms descending
over the rest of me who is the young
children in my shelter who grow
up under my leaves and rain
In our own shade
we embrace each other gravely &
look out tenderly upon the world

seeking only contemporaries
and speech and light, no father.

hold fast in arms before astonished eyes
whom you must grasp throughout great changes
constant and receptive as a capital city

is now a fire	now a frozen hand
a rainstorm	white birds
a rotting log	a young boy
a savaged sheep	an indifference

a kind of seriousness,   a kind of rage

and through each transforming
yourself to be not here whose
body shapes a hundred lights a
glowing strip of absence, night's
noisy and particular who
vanishes with that flawless sense
of occasion I guess you'd have if
only I knew you at first light
leaving 'the wrong body', old, known

such face bones honeycombed sockets
of strained eyes outlined in warm

light aching wrapped in impermeable
coating of pleasure going off wild

on the light-headed train   'will write
& write what there is beyond anything'

it is the 'spirit' burns in &
through 'sex' which we know about

saying 'It's true', I won't place or
describe it   It *is* & refuses the law

assume a country
held by small walls

assume a landscape
with lakes & the need for protection

assume a house
with shut doors and a fire

the house in the landscape
which roads irradiate

the hand the rocks the cradle
erect at every crossroads

*

not liking as mirrored
but likeness, activity

a whole life for likeness
after the silence

and does try and will try
and the past weight and the future

[15]

From NO FEE
(1978)

In 1970

The eyes of the girls are awash with violets
pansies are flowering under their tongues
they are grouped by the edge of the waves and are anxious to swim;
each one is on fire with passion to achieve herself.

Affections must not

This is an old fiction of reliability

is a weather presence, is a righteousness
is arms in cotton

this is what stands up in kitchens
is a true storm shelter
& is taken straight out of colonial history, master and slave

arms that I will not love folded nor admire for their 'strength'
linens that I will not love folded but will see flop open
tables that will rise heavily in the new wind & lift away, bearing their precious burdens

of mothers who never were, nor white nor black
mothers who were always a set of equipment and a fragile balance
mothers who looked over a gulf through the cloud of an act & at times speechlessly saw it

inside a designation there are people permanently started to bear it, the not-me against sociology

inside the kitchens there is realising of tightropes

milk, if I do not continue to love you as deeply and truly as you want and need

that is us in the mythical streets again

support, support

the houses are murmuring with many small pockets of emotion

on which spongy grounds adults' lives are being erected & paid for daily

while their feet and their children's feet are tangled around like those of fen larks

in the fine steely wires which run to and fro between love & economics

affections must not support the rent

I.   neglect.   the house

Work

For a time self-evident light all tremendously clear
to be sat down under in abstract triumph, still shaking with
luck and nearly-wasn't; later a flood of in this case loosestrife
dead wood dead children billowing in moondaisies set to
piped music tears and dreadful violence, only tolerable years later
through aesthetics to make red noons of what was at the time real blood.
So it goes on asserting the unbearable solid detail as real work, Lissitsky:
'work must be accepted

as one of the functions of the living organism
in the same way as the beating of the heart
or the activity of the nerve centres

so that it will be afforded the same protection'
and no sleep pricks out clear and small
people in landscapes who are pushing up around the sides of larger things.
Dear attention; fix that point precisely where
landscapes first got peopled & painting set off on a series of humane
journeys south to Venice; so for saints to be warming their hands at lions
on khaki mountains; netted camels to be arching home midfield,
black light and cliffs of rain to be taking their time across horizons
and an evil to heave itself out of a brown pond, foreground, unobserved.
Look out, saint. Not to be your own passions' heroine
else, invented, you'll stick in them. So, telegram: forget.

Not what you think

wonderful light
viridian summers
deft boys
no thanks

From DRY AIR
(1985)

Versions of three poems by Friedrich Hölderlin

The Ages

You towns of Euphrates!
You streets of Palmyra!
You forests of pillars
in wastes of the plain
what are you? You passed
beyond breathing, your crowns
snatched by smoke, by
divinity's flame.
Now I sit under clouds
each has its own peace
under well-arranged oaks
on the heath of the deer
and strange and dead to me
the souls of the blest.

(*'Lebensalter'*)

Each day I take . . .

Each day I take a different path
now to the river, now the wood
or to the rocks where roses are

I climb the hill where I look out
but find you nowhere in the light
my beauty, and my words are gone
into the air. Our words were right.

Yes, you are far away; your face
and clear sounds of your life are lost.
Where are the songs that brought me peace?
This man's grown old; the earth lacks grace.

Go well. Each day my restless mind
goes out to you, is turned away.
My eyes strain after you to see
lightly straight through to where you stay.

('Wohl geh' ich täglich')

Home

Happy the sailor, home to his still river
from far-off islands where he's worked.
I would like a home to reach
though what but sadness have I earned?

You river banks, you brought me up;
now can you calm the hurts of love?
Woods of my childhood, will you give
me peace of mind if I return?

('Die Heimat')

History

can we revolt to con the man
the idiot taurus won't let be

the candour of the marzipan
hermaphrodité's silvery ways

night took us by surprise
sparkling slowly with tears

Our youth and mine

Can years and years of folding in to the rumoured heart of / be in vain? as each
you repeats *you* in a clearer light, more amazed untiring openings
in the shine of this-face-only, the long astonished soft whistle
at speech known, can the most elaborate
swing out at last into a flat lit day? Say it could –
a tortuous road, that, to go down & back to here, like one of those zen riddles
you can guess the end of anyway –
love looked-for & returning like rain
& as randomly dispersed to a thousand equally radiant faces
as broad and unparticular as grass.
No time or characters in being happy, but each fresh angel's
the split image of that guest you'd long forgotten, & would have sworn was not

& still the immediate travelling problem, that there really *is* separation, geography,
& gets no younger (so wearing out in place I don't look up
but hear the sky raked by fortunates who are going away)
with you in the town of x where myself arrives
a good day later than my body on the train
while my imagination's entertained itself a whole week in advance
but at the last moment fights shy of getting incorporated –

[31]

how then ever to coincide? but sometimes it *does* work,
namelessly, and that's alive as can be.

Who ageing through local acts peopled by the persons of the drama
is fixed at the sites of institutionalised pain,
of which yes, you can have as much as you like
you can remember everything said that killed you, you are word-perfect
28 years of rehearsing got it off by heart for you
you examine it each night lovingly where it is all yours all for always
and it is a bright animal that rises in your sleep
each morning it swims neat as an eel between the wet dishes
small face, it will pick you out at the playground gates
or you could take it out with you to meetings, there are crowds
and you can become their violence with an easy permission

and here is the Madonna, she is professionally sad
she has had her day which has quite done for her, the Child
is separate and smiles. And this spreadeagled woman here
is not merely outlined in knives, but has in fact been pierced and has died of that.

Everything you think meets and rushes forward from many different directions
loudly all at once in a glow and a shout, knee-deep in pound notes.

[32]

Mastering the art of English art

In the gardens of the Villa Doria Pamphili
it's about this and about that;
more and more blue, those classical ladies,
looking like rain, the Fiats go streaming over the bridge.

No, not enough

Not enough sleep again
narrows your eyes.
Oh thirty-three.

Ah, so

Speaking apart, I hear my voice run on
In the red heart of an ear, an ear coils round me
disturb the text; you don't disturb the world

This train is inserted across England, its country
get a sense of history   of history

I found some change in my trouser pocket, like a man

What I do

An even time
all to myself, though
lately it hasn't been,
more violent. My
death will still
skip on, 'This way,
my love'. I know
but privately
I cross my heart; that
shakes, though, the noise-maker.
I am in several cupboards
deep, and wish well out,
wish out from this
dark air of china.
Is my name 'skeleton'
or only 'cup'?
A crack of light falls round me.

No

All the towels are red
the navy towel and the black
blood-soaked
and the white dress has slipped
to the bloodied floor.

This one you lose you could not love.
You were deceived, your flat blood knew
to open its bright factual eye.
This that you leak you never grew.

The officer is at the scarlet door.
Here is his evidence. Some body lied.
That body's mine but I am it.
And I am it and I have lied.

To the fields

Walking on grass
my friend ahead, I
behind with
the child. She
couldn't keep up
and wouldn't. The light
drained everything of
colour, the cattle
and pale daisies. I
didn't know his
mind then. By
evening, families
strung out across
the fields for
cars and homes
and we too

The ambition to advise speaks

'Do not be charmed by the long arch of your own trajectory
but shoot along boldly on the hard gaze of the straight

put yourself on the margins but don't be endlessly naming them
be taken with yourself if you are but keep quiet about it
& choose yourself a gender but be prepared to be flexible here

clear colour will be a help in this
say no to sociology always
in any event you will need music

remembering not to think yourself happy until you are
                                        which you will know
then go for it'

The ambition to not be particular speaks

'I cannot tell what gives each voice its tune –
some furious tenderness of buried words
or interference from the streets
and their hazardous crying –

but if for me some words must be exhumed
out of their sunken heat they must be cooled
to the grace of being common –

so to achieve my great colourlessness
I dive into the broken brilliant world
and float in it unindividuated, whitely'

No work in Britain; working abroad

A piece of sky scratches my bare leg.
It is bright blue chicory flowers
angled down the school road.
Now in my homeland they are all asleep.

*

Where have you got to?
This is all extraordinary.

I'm private
here, & write by the window.

Bedroom clouds.
Azaleas. Objects.
Different days.

*

The hot singing forests
and the air of democracy.
Lost men at the gates. Black
sharp shrubs and eucalypts
on the sweet plateaux are
shining in waves.

*

Glacial blue gleam
cliffs. Sonorous water
off Charing Cross Bridge and
then lift your eyes.

How many towns
I lean across, wandering.

*

Red fields, red soil
or tawny soil.
Small trees like gum
trees run through soft light.
There is all day, all
day to go.

*

The sea springs from the marsh
in a violet wedge.

A fine black gauze
veils the sky over
before your eyes.

*

Some trees
And a corner of the institution.

Where are dark cities, friends,
my native daughter.

From MOP MOP GEORGETTE
(1993)

Laibach Lyrik: Slovenia, 1991

*The milky sheen of birch trees
stepping forward. Breathless
the deeper woods.*

*Goldfinches rattle down
through branches, leap
and sparkle off to dusk.*

*Below a mass of cloud this evening
a faintly orange light
slides on your lifting smile.*

*Afternoon's blue winds dropped
now wreaths of raspberry smoke
pat the steady sky.*

*Cream fields chat quietly
careless of distant provinces
and the guns of rebels.*

*Whooping cranes rise where
herdsmen, clattering, wheel about
the plains in scarlet.*

Cut the slavonics now. Cut the slavonics.
Slovenian and all other civil planes are off.
The federal airforce has the skies sewn up.
The snows come early, Austrian lorries slide
across the mountain pass in slow veers sidelong
skate gingerly to fates, grand destinies dreamily chosen.
Entering Yugoslavia we aren't there, we are straight into Slovenia instead
late at night, frozen, instantly crazy with obsessive and terrible tenderness
again, unable to find my passport. Napoléon, sauveur of Illyria ! whose
monument in Ljubljana spells out in gleams of gold calligraphy, Our Liberty.
Here videos of the summer bombings, entitled the Triumph of Slovenia, or
How a Nation Awoke, are wrapped in paper jackets showing fighter planes
with yellow extension-lead cables, mortar smoke, on stalls with t-shirts,
logos of the state. The country restaurant pipes a first-time go
at national music to its dining rooms, unclear what that should sound like;
oompah Bavarian results, mortifying to the city friends, who disconnect
its speakers, drawing down a ruddy glare of sausages, peasant style.
Rain darkens the fish-scale roofs of the provincial capital. In London
temporary exiles meet, some in despair about their forced new names
others worn down with dislocation, with explaining histories
to well-meant local ignorant evenhandedness. A girl calls out 'This time
last year, we none of us knew or cared. The cars streamed down all summer
to the Dalmatian coast from Serbia, and so what. Did I grow up for this

[46]

to take new designations, learn to hate my neighbours, just because of where
I came from, which I never used to know? The last war stopped
before my mother's birth. Who says I must be 'Bosnian' now.
I grew up Yugoslavian. Just stop this craziness, these killings.' Another,
older, says 'It is a lie that walls are coming down in Europe. We see them rise
and we are penned inside. The deaths of twenty thousand make me this
that I don't want to be. But that blood lost means I must take that name –
though not that politics – must be, no not a nationalist, yet ambiguously Croatian
must be it through the dictates of those deaths alone. We should, all should –
look forward, must rebuild . . .' She stops. I'm seeing present history
glance round it for support, I'm hearing it at work to stammer its imperfect story
go on too long, be conscientious, grab at straws, then reach its edge of tears.

I'm not these, never could be, am by accident of place of birth protected, yet exactly as
this nation-sheltered onlooker, must try to think. The room splits into clumps and fights.
Outsiders now move off, get back to native non-community, and across real distances
made semi-manageable through irony; so that I'll say I've stood here
as a dark stand of trees, still, sealed black, outwardly silent but vibrantly
loud inside with others' gossip about itself, like 'the unconscious'; and I'll leave
as I might leave a party whose guests were venomous yet inconsolable, deliberately
straightening my shoulders and saying aloud, although to nobody in particular, It's good
to get some air. The usual spectator's cocky journey home through stupidness.
This evening's tongues go scrapping on till dawn:

The settling scar agrees to voice
what seems to speak its earliest cut.
A rage to be some wholeness gropes

past damage that it half recalls –
where it was, I will found my name.
A hesitant gap now stretches its

raw mouth: I will become this sex
and Istrian. And still at night
hair dazzles in white lights

from flares. A greenish patina
may roughen these spent shells
for future curious songs. Now people

and their resonant cities are obliterated.
What is it that shapes us, whether
we will or no, that through these

opened and reopened mouths that form
the hollow of a speaking wound, we
come to say, yes, now we are Illyrian.

Letters from Palmer

On moors the dark is spangled furze. Dusk noise presses.
Water *varnishes* everything that it covers, as pebbled beds
of streams. The plainly liquid quality of all shadow.

A blind baby feeling for the breast knows the taste of milk.
Woods must be rich, in thickly tumbling light.
Real tree colour, not anything picture colour.

The glimmering-through of the white paper.
Those thousand little luminous eyes which peer
through a finished linear etching, even in its shadows.

They have built us up with great houses, and destroyed
the elasticity of the air. How should the light strain through.
Guineas are being lost by the hundreds, in losing the Spring.

Interest is a capital lever when goodness moves it.
In May a peculiar grey effect is very charming.
If a man gets a name as a mannerist it is all up with him.

Enough of green tea poetry and smoky philosophy.
The choir of greys between violet and copper.
Keeping my shadows tender clear and neutral.

Vapour suspended over the far distance like a curtain.
I saw it in nature for so long that I was afraid to try it.
I have finished the little town by the blue river.

Small specks of pure white paint may glitter like the rain.
When I have gone to school to a potato in black & white chalk
I have found it difficult to make it unmistakably like.

As through a little frame a curtained spectacle
of downs and elms and matted pines. Stopping
the figure feeling intruding on the landscape feeling.

The upper shadows of objects in the air. The cool
sub-light they get from the sky. Moon-powdered
woollen leaves. The hillocks blocked in surges.

Where is the Vergilian muse? At the railway whistle she fled for ever.
Her very oxen wander the city disconsolate.
Corydon and Thyrsis meet in corduroys and Manchester cottons.

If I seem mirthful it is tinsel & spangles on a black ground.
O for a safe passage to that world where undivorced beauty
shall ever be the index and form of goodness.

Our earth is honeycombed with cells of fire. We suffer
the Poles to fight themselves out & the Danes & the Circassians
and need not expect pity when our turn comes.

Crude flake white is in hue a cold colour. Writing our
difficulties. I spring upon my books. You want something
which will not be taken away. Which will fill your heart.

Writhing for the death of my son. They may be allowed
to walk unseen as our guides in this darkness. You lay the book
down as tenderly as if you had handled something alive.

To come to the point, avoiding the temptation to impertinent
& superfluous labour. Exactness the common honesty of art.
What is prosperity without it but a violated responsibility.

The stove within me rages. A filmless sun burns. In cobalt air.
Hills fired with living gold. I am walked and scorched to death.
Drenched in a hot white mist. Grand coruscation of sudden light.

The solemn & inexhaustible eloquence of rains and mountain.
O the playful heave and tumble of lines in the hills here.
We are first green and then grey and then nothing in this world.

A shortened set

All the connectives of right recall
have grown askew. I know
a child could have lived, that
my body was cut. This cut
my memory half-sealed but glued
the edges together awry.
The skin is distorted, the scar-tissue
does damage, the accounts are wrong.
And this is called 'the healing process'.
Now nothing's aligned properly.
It's a barbarous zone.
The bad sutures
thicken with loss and hope –
brilliant, deliberate
shaking patients in an anteroom
refusing the years, ferocious to be called
so I'll snip through the puckered skin
to where they tug for re-aligning. Now
steady me against inaccuracy, a lyric urge
to showing-off. The easy knife
is in my hand again. Protect me.

Small is the history, and dark.
Its purplish valleys are unfurled
as the militant trees clash over it together.
I'd long in its steep descent to slip
past fuss and toughness to escape
both well-oiled grief and an escaper's
cheery whistling. Tedious. This
representing yourself, desperate to get it right,
as if you could, is that the aim of the writing?
'I haven't got off lightly, but I got off' – that won't
deflect your eyes that track you through the dark.
There is the traveller, there the decline
and his sex that the journey strips from him. A
perfectly democratic loneliness sets out
down the mined routes of speaking to its life.
So massively, gently, should it go
that it might overtake
even the neatest Professor of Speed.

The last sun on dark red brick burns violet-black where
I wait to get back something in the narrows of the city
under its great sides, whose brick or painted walls
glow into the paler light above them, a hugely quiet halo
formed from the internal heat of rooftops. These seep
their day off to the sky cupped very coolly distant
over this tight rim. My heart takes grateful note
to be in life, the late heat shaped in bricks of air
stuck out, hot ghosts to catch my hand on.
The slap of recognition that you know.
Your feelings, I mean mine, are common to us all:
that puts you square between relief and boredom
under the standoffish sky.
In this I'm not unique, I'm just
the only one who thinks I'm not. Maybe.

How can black paint be warm? It is. As ochre
stains slip into flooding milk, to the soft black
that glows and clots in sooty swathes.
Its edges rust, it bleeds lamp-black
slow pools, as planes of dragged cream
shoot over it to whiteness, layered.
Or the cream paint, leaden, wrinkles: birch bark
in slabs, streaked over a peeling blue. A twist
of thought is pinned there. A sexual black. And I
can't find my way home. Yet wandering there I may.
By these snow graphics. Ice glazed
to a grey sheen, hard across dark grass spikes.

Is that what's going on – the slow
replacement of a set of violent feelings
by neutral ones. The hell if so.
There has been damage, which must stop at me.
I think that's finished. Then the underside
of a brushed wing unsettles things.
I'd cup that powdery trace in mind
like a big moth in a matchbox, whirring.

Are you alright I ask out there
straining into the dusk to hear.
I think its listening particles of air
at you like shot.
You're being called across your work
or – No I don't want that thought.
Nor want to get this noise to the point
it interests me. It's to you. Stop.

But

Am I alright, you don't ask me.
Oh probably, and in the heart
of this light on hills it is for me
alone to speak. No triumph.

This milky light's a fact and the broad air
and the strip of primrose water, a long way down.
That red dot is my car, let's go
Or let I go.

⸺

– That black dot was myself.
I strike you as complete:
a late unpacking in life
in hope of a human view.
After these nights of rain on
the mountain the water's running
so hard it's marbled white
the streams like heavy snow.
Deletions are sifting down
onto the study floor – Cut
more cut more, mutter my
hearing creatures, snouts
rooting upward for light.
They push to nudge my
failures aside and go but
what would become of me in
the quiet once they were out.
Will you be good towards
these animals of unease
I can just about call them home.

Coffee goes coppery on my tongue today
as 'Let's Dance' is hammered out again on the radio.
It was my party and I wept not wanting to.
'Mother of children, don't go into the house in the dark'.
Letters crash onto the hall floor with their weight of intelligence
                                          and junk.
I get up with hope for them, until word may finally arrive.

It is called feeling but is its real name thought?
Moons in their spheres are not so bland as these.
A round O says I feel and all agree.
Walking by many on London streets
in a despair which carries me
I look from face to face like a dog going
in the social democracy of loneliness.
May move instead through a shimmer
around me of racial beauty crying like something expensive
which breaks into eyes sparkling all over skin.

It's that simple
in another town.
No, it doesn't know me
nor this train I'm on.

The ex-poet's beside herself:
'Here in the clouded
red, the grey, the burnt
oak forest, the rails shake'.

Safely I'll love it by letter
yet skip the 'better
that way' to cancel
the doubter's rhyme, trembling.

Aha we are frozen
stiff as young hyacinths —
outrageous blue
decides to leave green.

I'd drive anywhere with anyone, just
to have that held sense of looking out
from a container, amiably, stolidly, while
I'm portered by. Along the ring-road
murmurous orange lights on stilts with
necks stuck out like herons on the grey
slipway, angled above the cars repeating
themselves fast and fast as if they were one.
When I'm unloaded and stood in dread
at home encircled by my life, whose
edges do show – then I so want it to run
and run again, the solitary travelling perception.
Road movie: Protectedness, or, Gets through time.

An ice blue calm, violently sustained,
has got to know a thing about this nation
and our being in it.
How do I act, then, properly
without a sticky modesty
in the crammed-fullness of the place
too dense for story threads to pierce?
I'm quiet. I'm at the end of all opinion.
Should I not know where clearness lies.
Time has run short and I need company
to crack my separate stupidity. I'd thought
to ask around, what's lyric poetry?
Its bee noise starts before I can:
You do that; love me; die alone.

Don't quote the 'we'
of pairs, nor worse, of sentient
humanity, thanks.

That's attitudinising, in those
three lines. That's what I do.
Help me out of it, you
you sentient humanity.

I was signed up for a course
on earth by two others who left me and
left me impossibly slow at Life Skills

at admitting unlikeness or grasping the
dodgem collision whose shock isn't
truth but like the spine says is no

deception. I hate the word
'collusion' used of love but in the end
I wasn't anyone else ever –

that I sweated blood to force
lucidity to come as if headlocked
by history, to explain I really was –

all that was powered by desperation –
the thought of it makes me mortified.
Then after years, so-whattish:

The loves are returned to
themselves, leaving
an out post-sexual.

Unanxious, today.
A feeling of rain
and dark happiness.

Rain slops into dust
caught underfoot
in short grit runnels.

Faint news from the wharf
peppered on skin in
fresh patters of rain.

The evening lightens.
A friend's shout
blown inaudibly.

Sit. See, from the riverside
winds buzz new towers
of puzzling wealth.

Curved to this view
the gleam of a moment's
social rest.

Hair lit to a cloud
the sunlight lowering
first hesitant then strong.

In a rush
the glide of the heart
out on a flood of ease.

Summer

Looking in pools to see things flick.
Red globules. A million navy lips,
pursed mussels.

Lean in a head wind – 'spread-eagled'
should not pin down, should soar
but biscuit rocks stare over water.

*

Night falls like a coin in a slot ambling
down tiers of perspex trays
tipped to Animal Aid.

Moon, its pre-industrial light. What though
the dark thee cumber:
Glow, worm. Say to her.

Wherever you are, be somewhere else

A body shot through, perforated, a tin sheet
beaten out then peppered with thin holes,
silvery, leaf-curled at their edges; light flies

right through this tracery, voices leap, slip side-
long, all faces split to angled facets: whichever
piece is glimpsed, that bit is what I am, held

in a look until dropped like an egg on the floor
let slop, crashed to slide and run, yolk yellow
for the live, the dead who worked through me.

Out of their lined shell the young snakes broke
past skin fronds stretched over sunless colour or
lit at a slant, or saturated grey – a fringe flapping

round nothing, frayed on a gape of glass, perspex
seen through, seen past, no name, just scrappy
filaments lifting and lifting over in the wind.

Draw the night right up over my eyes so that I
don't see and then I'm gone; push the soft hem
of the night into my mouth so that I stay quiet

when an old breeze buffets my face to muffle
me in terror of being left, or is that a far worse
terror of not being left. No. Inching flat out

over a glacier overhanging blackness I see no
edge but will tip where its glassy cold may stop
short and hard ice crash to dark air. What do

the worms sing, rearing up at the threshold?
Floating a plain globe goes, the sky closes.
But I did see by it a soul trot on ahead of me.

I can try on these gothic riffs, they do make
a black twitchy cloak to both ham up and so
perversely dignify my usual fear of ends.

To stare at nothing, just to get it right
get nothing right, with some faint idea of
this as a proper way to spend a life. No, what

I really mean to say instead is, come back
won't you, just all of you come back, and give
me one more go at doing it all again but doing it

far better this time round – the work, the love stuff –
so I go to the word-processor longing for line cables
to loop out of the machine straight to my head

and back, as I do want to be only transmission –
in sleep alone I get articulate, to mouth the part of
anyone and reel off others' characters until the focus

of a day through one-eyed self sets in again: go into it.
I must. *The flower breaks open to its bell of sound
that rings out through the woods.* I eat my knuckles

hearing that. I've only earned a modern, what, a flatness.
Or no, I can earn nothing, but maybe
some right to stop now and to say to you, Tell me.

– That plea for mutuality's not true. It's more ordinary that
flying light should flap me away into a stream of specks
a million surfaces without a tongue and I never have wanted

'a voice' anyway, nor got it. Alright. *No silver coin has been*
nailed to your house's forehead you dog-skin among the fox fur
where did you get that rosewater to make your skin so white ?

I did get that rosewater before I came to the light grass
shakes in a wind running wild over tassels of barley
the sails were of the light green silk sewn of both gold

and white money, take down take down the sails of silk set up
the sails of skin and something dark and blurred upon the ground
where something else patrols it, cool, nervous, calling out

Stop now. Hold it there. Balance. Be beautiful. Try.
– And I can't do this. I can't talk like any of this.
You hear me not do it.

Lure, 1963

Navy near-black cut in with lemon, fruity bright lime green.
I roam around around around around acidic yellows, globe
oranges burning, slashed cream, huge scarlet flowing
anemones, barbaric pink singing, radiant weeping When
will I be loved? Flood, drag to papery long brushes
of deep violet, that's where it is, indigo, oh no, it's in
his kiss. Lime brilliance. Obsessive song. Ink tongues.
Black cascades trail and spatter darkly orange pools
toward washed lakes, whose welling rose and milk-
beribboned pillars melt and sag, I'm just a crimson
kid that you won't date. Pear glow boys. Clean red.
Fluent grey green, pine, broad stinging blue rough
strips to make this floating space a burning place of
whitest shores, a wave out on the ocean could never
move that way, flower, swell, don't ever make her blue.
Oh yes I'm the great pretender. Red lays a stripe of darkest
green on dark. My need is such I pretend too much, I'm
wearing. And you're not listening to a word I say.

A misremembered lyric

A misremembered lyric: a soft catch of its song
whirrs in my throat. 'Something's gotta hold of my heart
tearing my' soul and my conscience apart, long after
presence is clean gone and leaves unfurnished
no shadow. Rain lyrics. Yes, then the rain lyrics fall.
I don't want absence to be this beautiful.
It shouldn't be; in fact I know it wasn't, while
'everything that consoles is false' is off the point –
you get no consolation anyway until your memory's
dead; or something never had gotten hold of
your heart in the first place, and that's the fear thought.
Do shrimps make good mothers? Yes they do.
There is no beauty out of loss; can't do it –
and once the falling rain starts on the upturned
leaves, and I listen to the rhythm of unhappy pleasure
what I hear is bossy death telling me which way to
go, what I see is a pool with an eye in it. Still let
me know. Looking for a brand-new start. Oh and never
notice yourself ever. As in life you don't.

Shantung

It's true that anyone can fall
in love with anyone at all.
Later, they can't. Ouf, ouf.

How much mascara washes away each day
and internationally, making the blue one black.
Come on everybody. Especially you girls.

Each day I think of something about dying.
Does everybody? do they think that, I mean.
My friends! some answers. Gently
unstrap my wristwatch. Lay it face down.

Knowing in the real world

A yellow glow slips from the brick houses.
Some steely clouds swell up over them.

One afternoon hour burns away until a rust-
coloured light sinks in towards evening

or any time at all when I fall straight through
myself to thud as onto the streaked floor of

a swimming pool drained out for winter, no
greeny depths but lined in blackened leaves.

Then the cold comes to tighten the air. In my room
I hear cars and the snow flying around the street.

I'm not outside anything; I'm not inside it either.
There's no democracy in beauty, I'm following

human looks. Though people spin away, don't
be thrown by their puzzling lives, later the lives

secrete their meaning. *The red sun's on the rain.*
Where do I put myself, if public life's destroyed.

Only to manage something blindingly sweet. I'm
too old now to want to be careful. Then I wasn't.

What you see is what you could have easily. You
could. Or take me home. Another kind of thought,

liquid behind speech, bleeds away from it altogether.
I washed my son in the morning milk.

Sliced into the shine of now, a hand on a blade.
A wound, taproot in its day, its red blossom in light.

The wind sheets slap the sea to ruffled wheat-fields.
Angel, fish, paradise, rain of cherries.

Poem beginning with a line from Proverbs

As iron sharpens iron
I sharpen the face of my friend
so hard he sings out
in high delicate notes.

A struggle for mastery to most speak
powerful beauty would run any
attention or kindness clean out
of town in angry rags.

Ringed by darkness the heart pulsates.
And power comes in like lightning.
A lion in the room, fair and flowing
twists with unsparing eyes.

Whitely the glance runs
to it and away. But let it
talk its golden talk if we
don't understand it.

Grabbed by remote music
I'm frightening myself. Speak
steadily as is needed to
stare down beauty. That calms it.

Lyric

Stammering it fights to get
held and to never get held
as whatever motors it swells
to hammer itself out on me

then it can call out high
and rounded as a night-
bird's cry falling clean
down out of a black tree.

I take on its rage at the cost of
sleep. If I love it I sink
attracting its hatred. If I
don't love it I steal its music.

Take up a pleat in this awful
process and then fold me flat
inside it so that I don't see
where I'm already knotted in.

It is my burden and subject
to listen for sweetness in hope
to hold it in weeping ears though
each hurt each never so much.

What else

A clean historical wind has cut
the forest, torn it to streaming
ribbons.   Now under its snapped
branches I'll listen for silence.

At first I'll hear only my blood
ticking on inside my eardrums.
Failing light lays its hand over my lips.
Breathing darkness presses forward.

It will rush in from a great way off
to put its mouth to my straining ears.
This time I'll know it as death, I'll cup
my hands round its conviction.

It will come sobbing in my ears
calling my names to me over and over.
I'll think, and try to keep my eyes
wide open as if swimming underwater.

But I don't know how at the time
I'll conduct myself on that forest floor
where I will be quite alone. So
somebody here, hurry, take part in life.

Song

Some very dark blue hyacinths on the table
A confession or two before dusk
flings open the fridge with loud relief
Listen honey I . . .

A warm disturbing wind cruises the high road

where in curtained rooms children
are being beaten, then so am I again but no one's
asking for it, I'm asking for something different now

When it's time to go

When an aggressively uncontrolled schadenfreude
reads a personal threat in everywhere
and so animatedly takes this as 'the political'
that the very kitchen colander shells out a neat
wehrmacht helmet of brown rice
das schmeckt nach mehr!
or when an inverse brand of professional unhappiness
taps on its wristwatch 'as a realist I . . .' – then

set this boy free

No this isn't me, it's just my motor running

O great classic cadences of English poetry
We blush to hear thee lie
Above thy deep and dreamless.

True North

My body's frame, arched to a drum, houses a needle. A splinter of this world
has stuck in me, snapped-off, afloat down syrupy blood. It points me on.
This thick body can't dim its brilliance though it vexes the car of my flesh.
Sliver of outside that I cradle inside and which guarantees me my life also.

Rayon

The day is nervous buff – the shakiness, is it inside the day or me?
Perhaps the passions that we feel don't quite belong to anyone
but hang outside us in the light like hoverflies, aping wasps and swivelling
and lashing up one storm of stripes. In tiny cones of air.
Yet you enact that feeling, as you usually   *bzzzzzzzz*   get to do it, while I,
I do this. If it takes me all night and day. Oh Carol.

Marriage song with a remembered line

The partridge is possessed of the earth it runs on
As the deep clouds possess the sea.
The blue-black. The
Catastrophic rain.
And slowly fall down together over and over

Poor Snow

The violet
light of snow falling.

Its tiny darts
make eye stripes.

Dark flakes
rapid, upwards.

It's restless, it can't
find whiteness.

Its grey and violet
trillion souls.

Pastoral

Gents in a landscape hang above their lands.
Their long keen shadows trace peninsulas on fields.
Englishness, Welshness, flow blankly out around them.
Hawks in good jackets lean into the wind, shriek 'lonely I:
This sight is mine, but I can't think I am.
Those pale blue floods of watered silk have flounced indoors, I hear
their flick of vicious fans. I'll land and stow my feathered legs
and walk to find a sweet interior of beer' — These men are right:
it's hard to own perceptions setting out and in, but
settling with a shudder into a hired car as if into a coat
or bed, Rose Riley in the back, our lives in the hand of my calm
crossing the bealach past implausible farms and up and up the
breathless track of couldn't reverse now if I had to, I've not
had enough of this yet. Look out for those in our red car
so that it may be well; the road thread spins
out of the car's smooth mouth, a dream of ease slips back —

I don't know why it isn't any harder than this
I don't know why this light is evident
I fell into sleep, and that was a pure place
I woke, it is so easy that I can only smile —

A homely accident will do for that: so within days
I've one eye left that pulls to join the darkness
in which its brother sits; one eye's unharmed
yet I can't steer by that, my brain
would drag the shutters down, now that the dark

has got the balance. I, snowman, cinder for eye
bandaged white upon red, an icon of d.v.,
must tap my blindfold way around
this mother-and-child, child-and-mother
silver hoop that I live in; who
will step in to help me. Inside the eye
taped closely shut, repeating suns
are fringed with cloud and race away
into each other, and as they hotly go
from brown to reddish-violet to ochre
they snake, like sunspot photographs
or lights which stream out from eclipsed moons;
they'll not keep still but whoosh and whoosh
in a poor video I can't switch off. The iris
is frayed insect wings; what if the
pupil's black should slop and run across its
sheeny brown and green, what if that black
spill out of its neat rigorous circle –
I haven't got a body, till it hurts –
Eyes can mend fast: into the place of all of us
my sight returns and with it mastery
to track again the feather-trousered flights.

Well all right

Above, a flurry of swans, brothers, great wings airy
around my bowed head in rushing darkness, neatly
these bone fingers plaited their green cloaks each night
to unfeather them so now they stand upright before me
freed and gaily they leap to their caparisoned horses as
in my breathing cell I smooth down my own cloak of
nettles – but Grimm sweetie mediaeval Griseldas, right
out on the night plains are no tiny lights of huddlement
but only the impersonal stars in blackness and the long
long winds. What you see is what you see: it's never
what you won't. Well alright, things happened it would
be pleasanter not to recall, as a deeply embarrassed dog
looks studiedly at a sofa for just anything to do instead,
so determine to assume events silently with no fuss –
who doesn't try to – yes that is a dart in my neck and
doesn't it look a bit biedermeier – so take up that thud
of attack dropped out of a righteously wide-open beak
sailing slowly across its own high sky which you'd not
registered as contempt straight out to kill – far rather
than know that, wear it as an owned cloak's blazing
fabric stuck in the fine flesh of your shoulders like any
natural skin burning; so cloaked, no one sees through
to you wrapped in darkness, only a darkness pressed to
outward navy twill – no queen of the night's gorgeous
winking suit, just suave cheap unexceptional off any
rack – want to slip out of it? but flesh has soaked to join
its fiery choric costume. Break out in flames. Leap to

the crests of orange birds flickering along the long line
of shoulders, hiss, warble in gaping whistles hoarse lyre
chants of plumed and swollen throats whose glowing trills
waver and zigzag the swayed neck heavy under the flare
song of any body glittering with hard memory. Let fall
this garment with its noisy wings. Slide from me now –
and let's just run something red and stinging rapidly down
the page, shall we, let's try an echt gloss speed placing
let's stand back in triumph dripping brushes, shall we
see what can be made out of this lot my lot, its lovely
trailed gash wet as a frock in a pool, what it's for is for
defence, it will keep your beautiful soul glazed as a
skein of floating hill mist and as quietly as slightly
and as palely lit – at risk of frank indifference it may
make beauty to sleep and, or, to sleep with. Who sang
'you don't have to die before you live' – well who.

A drift

Move swift as a blur a fast drawn finger's smudge a
corner of the eye's unsteady streak a smear of nothing
solid only shaking fragments of tried-stopped-tried a
lot of noise which hurt nobody, keep head down keep
hands wrapped round head, jabbed down tight into eyes
ears keep blocked covered with hard fingers – to the north
you can run you can run till your feet glaze to the ground
miraculous ice particles keen out, chime, rattle in whipping
winds, carved face leans into stinging white of arctic night
a noble post for bears to circle with their amber urine in
the snow, no, shred drained mouth and toss the chattering
bits to any rapid driving lake to chop and drag them down
a tattered slipstream. Silenced drift. A cloud swims under
frozen waters, milky arch of wings, its shadow whirls
down screaming – how to a measured cool? if I lay down
my shield the loss-dread darts up flicking in my throat so
take me by the shoulders, steady me, a finger-tip could do
until some solidness wells back and if the sweet talk's going
to come why then I'll talk it though it's going to be raining
indoors: a bad law – what you need you shall not get until
once you no longer need it then you will, will fall through
jampacked rivers red with thickset fish, through thrashing
muscled rivers' noisy dash pulsing from mud depths up to
air-drenched jumping surfaces in brilliant scales of scarlet
time. I hear the calm talk nurse this power right in the teeth
of harm. Learn proper sexual pride and how that's placed.
These sentences come fast, give me no grief – does that mean

that their whole tone is false and that their flow slid out
of some cheap ease-machine? Oh how that man do howl.
Wait, lean from the topmost window, see over all this city
in its gravely vigorous life the moon hung orange in the
humming sky, the deeply breathing the electric air, tall
houses dropping glow, one fox-pure shriek, dark gardens'
charcoal pools, faint droning far-off traffic, never sleep
high twists of sirens spiral down the road and palest heads
of swimming roses gape awash in their own light against
the grind of buses starting out as in this night a single
traveller flies home through everything inside one life, its
fearful hesitations, pouncing leaps of speed; at daybreak
an hour's whiteness comes to lie in folds not brushed by
any shadow screens, I act as a fan, I find soul settlement.

Cruelty without beauty

Go on working around my hairline with a blade
and all you'll come to is a white sheen of bone
and all that would tell you is that I'm, what else,
human. I can tell you that now. Don't make
yourself into such a fine instrument of knowledge
that you slice uselessly back into your own hand
shocking yourself. There is a body, or soul, under
your skin too, but you won't assuage your doubts
about it by unpeeling me; no, that will uncover nothing
but your worse original anxiety. If I speak with formal
heaviness, that's the weight of stiff grief bending down
leaves, and the mild rain spotting their dust into rings.
No I don't much like this bland authoritative tone either
but it is what I took from years of reworded loss.
So if my skin slid downwards to the ground
you would see only a standing pillar of blood.
Believe that this would be true also of you.
– Such distanced care for self, rendered as knowing,
makes anybody ill: I'll drop this clinic voice to say
that this hot scowl of songs marks rage for
closeness just not found in a true human love –
burn, work, burn blue, since one clean word on
someone's blank makes salt well under any tongue,
am I to go unswollen, arm across my shoulders
good, that's who off the end of a wrist? so tired of
howling more more grand babe yet if there's angel too
this thick extent of longing's ugly as it's true. Heavy

water. Show your wound: Ah yes mine's deeper;
is that my shaming subject after all. Best get this
done on paper no one hears so I'll stay still in life
where I hear water speaking, may stand where light
falls as the plain light will – no that lot skims on wire
rhetoric, totters from tightly civic pause to weeping
open cut and back, but can't get balanced; its figure
sways with outflung arms, I do, to hold the deadly
wish to be white eye stripped out of human motion
as if sight crashed to clearness, clean of me:
brown rock and leaden sea. Crows in the wood
faced to the wind, pinned on high branches. Dark
blobs. Clacks on the wind. The drumming light.
Yet no one should say to me, Nothing's enough
for you, ever. But I do want to kill and die.

So is it?

Opening mouth up to sifting rain, blurred to an o,
crouched to the green wash, swooping water,
stone arches slit to wind-cropped turf, in a grip
turn as sea-slicing gannets cut shock fans of
white water. Held shudder, sluiced in low cloud.
Where is a steady place where work gets fairly done.
Straight speech can drop out from behind the teeth
or the hands shake out clean strokes from bunched
knots onto energetic white or long soft ropes of
line loop from the mouth, uncoil to columns
hollowed to poured sheen purity, only in shelter.
Some. I walk into a light hot wood. Inside it all
exhales, a sulky wind gets up, slings a sad mass
at the back of eyes lowered for chattering dusk,
fingers dried ochres in rough air brushed rustling
to cream hoops, strokes powdery blues tacked on
to black wire. Die deeper into life at every second.
And no self-coating slips onto my papers to make
them pulse to rooms emptied of me, they'll bear no
faint film for my children to wipe off later, so solidly
do objects stay themselves – the handwriting of the
freshly dead just doesn't get any loopier or more
archaic, as waxed comb honey would seep through
knuckles or pine ooze stiffen, domed to wasps.
Things packed with what they are. Not slatted I.
Preserve a self, for what? for ice through the ribs,
pale splinters driven straight to the heart's meat.

Calf of my senses. I'd thought out ways to grasp —
have walked straight off their edges. To dreams
of silent towns, nights, doorways, gazes, radios
on, while here a man turns and turns towards his
window, staring out over the street at dusk as rain-
hemmed curtains sway, their blackening yellowed
net. All seek a piercing charm to throb gingerly
nursed in our hands like a bird. Dear heart don't be
so strange to me but be nature. Or give me a sudden
bluish look. If I can get this far. An oil spill on the
wet road swims outwards, pleats, and flashes lilac or
rusting orange at its rim where it will dry and darken.
I think that's it. As I must think it is like this for you —
it is, isn't it. Don't tell me that edge that I never believe.

Dark looks

Who anyone is or I am is nothing to the work. The writer
properly should be the last person that the reader or the listener need think about
yet the poet with her signature stands up trembling, grateful, mortally embarrassed
and especially embarrassing to herself, patting her hair and twittering 'If, if only
I need not have a physical appearance! To be sheer air, and mousseline!'
and as she frets, the minute wars scorch on through paranoias of the unreviewed
herded against a cold that drives us in together – then pat me more, Coventry,
to fall from Anglo-Catholic clouds of drifting *we*'s high tones of feeling down
to microscopic horror scans of tiny shiny surfaces rammed up against the nose
cascading on Niagara, bobbed and jostled, racing rusted cans of Joseph Cotten reels
charmed with his decent gleam: once *we* as incense-shrouded ectoplasm gets blown
fresh drenched and scattered units pull on gloss coats to preen in their own polymer;

still it's not right to flare and quiver at some fictive 'worldly
through middle-aged hormonal pride of *Madame, one must bleed, it's necessary* . . .
Mop mop georgette. The only point of holding up my blood is if you'd think 'So what?
We've all got some of that': since then you'd each feel better; less apart. – Hardly:
it's more for me to know that I have got some, like a textbook sexual anxiety
while the social-worker poet in me would like her revenge for having been born and left.
What forces the lyric person to put itself on trial though it must stay rigorously uninteresting?
Does it count on its dullness to seem human and strongly lovable; a veil for the monomania
which likes to feel itself helpless and touching at times? Or else it backs off to get sassy
since arch isn't far from desperate: So, take me or leave me. No, wait, I didn't mean leave
me, wait, just *don't* – or don't flick and skim to the foot of a page and then get up to go –

[96]

Red Shout

Terrible to think it's more alive here when I'm
alone than when I'm not – that something might
come right just where 'the edges of a page begin
to bleed and show that it is human' – and come
more right than when I do the same – I see how
there could be an okay life whose feeling was
kept collared and pinned down only over the
writing – I still wait for a really human sign
as light and shocking as an annunciation –
sometimes I get it and in democratic form: *Red
Shout*. Red waves race by the sides of the eye
to open out beyond in tides of shining browns
sliced harder in to black and quicker as a sheet of
clear red beauty rips apart – if there's good power
this red won't stop but zips straight through
who's here flat out and glad, hit hard on the head
by life and through who isn't: all this means only
it can work, the corrective of in this case paint
for isolation – what works is just that someone
possibly scared stiff and also living did it, no?

Seven Strangely Exciting Lies

i Take two of these tablets tonight and in the morning go on living

So get up speed. So you're sick with fear again so what so what
Though in the past you screamed you wept you are still here alive.
Get up a head of speed and you may nip through rocks without quite getting smashed apart on them.
So you bit on iron until the blood ran out of your lips
So your eyes swam into dark blue clouds with the enormous misting shock of it
So you couldn't see your hands in front of you, you hardly knew how to breathe
yet you do take breath after breath, one by one you ease them all out carefully again
and then you take another, for someone else will tell you when it's time to stop, not you.
So you ground your forehead onto the concrete to skin yourself back into manageable life
because a streak of dusty red showed you could start a little harm and stop and then restart it
but you lived it, look into your eye at the shiny black life rolling around in it, get up

and breathe, just practising this will fill your life up steadily for months, while later on getting distracted is better – as on a long drive to the seaside when after tedious hours the upside-down triangle of navy blue is glimpsed, jammed hard into the V of the land and a glad cry goes up, the car-sick infant groans but she still gets reluctantly interested despite herself, and longs for sand and fish and chips and roundabouts again – next become mildly malicious in studying the failed consolations of middle age that at least some of the people you once mistakenly went to bed with and *v.v.* now sometimes look seedier, more despairing than you, though that's only because you get to use lipstick and hair-dye whereas they on the whole do not – your vanities, and pleasure in theatrical self-blame, have got you where you are today that's here: and though you've noticed now that you can breathe again, you do.

ii Glamour

Rattling through market racks of nineteen-fifties poplin
and sixties Suzie Wong dresses with grey-oiled necklines
labelled 'mandarin dresses' by their sellers born *circa* 1970
I *circa* 1948 still want to look, equals be, more alright
than I'll ever see myself. Or am. That doesn't stop
although by now it should – who does it stop for –
and the slow fight to get redeemed from the original sin
of having got born at all, can't that be over with by now?
Suzie woke up but to roughened brocade and under an eyelid
less like a milk-white nut, finds being seen a curse since I
can't demonstrate the measured blonde I truly am beneath
these awful curls: vulgar as this, I'm sagging with shopping
with how to hook on to the sliding skin of the world in time
or: in time I am going to die, can you be there

-iii Oleanna

I'd thought you'd get through any disagreement just by talking
by persisting quietly. Fool. Steel-rimmed the hole at the centre
through which all hopes of contact plummet down in flames
as modes of talk criss-cross from opposite directions like jets in flight
which rightly never slow or swerve to read the fleecy trails of others
then something searing wipes its arc across my sight again
as rape fields of acrylic flowers do stripe your eyeballs yellow
and unreflecting green takes charge at the horizon threatening to rain –
shove off or I soak you sunshine – suppose you stopped describing
something, would stopping free you from it, almost as if it hadn't happened?
So is that shiver down the back of the neck water, or is it memory calling water
or is it squaring up to getting properly shredded, which does cut clean away
from iron edges soaking into rust, from blurring fiery wells of tin-work –
someone calling tell them I'm not home, hurt me so bad to see my baby get
away, ashen-mouthed, smoking regret – instead of all that tactile surface junk
there is this sobbing flash, you-die immediacy: who longs for decent
and consensual talk, it is that calm and democratic front I'd work to be:
I was not born to that.

iv Lucille's tune

Riding this gorgeous car I saw in the wing-
mirror night-black leather coming up blind

it's the beginning it's the end of the world
though God knows I've wished it wasn't

an engine of light forgets about everything
but roaring you into it: blue drenches you

first they swear they'll love you to the grave
next they're down the woods to dig it for you:

little taffeta lips, call yourself a mother? *There
ain't nothing to you but I love you still,* don't

care that much for you and I always will.
You can hack off my breasts to write 'tits'

but you can't grow them on to your wire chest.
Starry unconscious: sea body: child maintenance

[102]

Not your natural-historical, your exacting tender mushroom gill accounting
Others once got their Observer books for seven and sixpence too
Nor your fragile translucent leaf trembling in its behold-me wonder
Which is a behold-you wonder

Not your landscapes stiffened with figurines of an ageing woman politician, it is harder than that
Not your happy here-we-go-down-together dream of a roseate catastrophe
Nor your reassuring conviction that whole governments
Will pale and stagger under the jawbones of your dismembered syntax.
Vain boy! it keeps you busy, though you know
That Belgrade and Zagreb still shelter many post-surrealists, as does East Central One.

What I want please write it for me
Since my not managing to
Makes me malicious as this new costume
As the curlicued tomb.
Now will some silent throat step up
Unlock a Marvell karaoke.

vi Flip, flop

What clicks and rattles coloured strings of plastic curtains all the afternoon.
What writes down 'vanish' and then worries that 'varnish' might have been
more truthful; at least prettier – from where I sit, exactly what's the difference between the
two? I have to know.

What is it that I inch down, like a mouse in the tranquil throat of a snake.
– Be quiet it's a kind of work isn't it, so work, eat flies, and love your children.
Although they too will leave you, they're always leaving you, you guano monument.

vii Disintegrate me

There was such brilliance lifting off the sea, its aquamarine strip
blocked in behind white-dashed mimosas, that it stung my eyes
all morning as I stood in the old playground, pushing the swing
steadily, looking out across the water and longing to do without

these radio voices, and without my post as zealous secretary, as
transmitter of messages from the dead, who'd issue disclaimers
that they'd ever sent them – all the while a slow hot cut spreads
to baste me now with questions of my own complicity in harm
muttering thoughtfully about 'patterns' until I'm stamped out as
an old paisley shawl or worn kelim, do I look good as this one
or should I be less loud, or less repetitive? and on the top of my
wardrobe, familiar spirits cluster and hang to chatter, lean over
to peer down interestedly at me, vivaciously complaining about
the large amounts of fluff I've left up there, 'that's just as we'd
expect': meanwhile the out-to-kill person is not, or so she or he
shrugs, pulled at by voices, but dead at heart stands amnesiac
plumped out with the effective innocence of the untroubled –
This gloss is taking me on unconvincing dashes down blind
alleys I mistrust since, desperate to see things straight, I can't fit
apt blame in to self-damnation: could I believe instead in drained
abandon, in mild drift out over some creamy acre studded with
brick reds, to be lifted, eased above great sienna fields and borne
onward to be an opened stem or standing hollow, a flesh ring
through which all slips or a fluent cylinder washed through by
azure-tangled braid, trailing Stella Maris, fervent star of the sea

marine milk vessel flopped at the lip flicking down swathes of
gulls emulsifying blackened earth striped and coiled under rock
under burnt straw air fuzzed in breathy fields of coconut-sharp
gorse flowers flushed tan on cliffs where lower, toothpaste green
lucidly rears and rears in the crash of blinding crumpled water
smoothing to clear and flat; so calmly let me disperse so simply
let me disperse, drawn out thin-frothed in a broad lacy pancake
fan of salt, or let me fall back as dolphins rock back in the sea
twirled like slow toys on pin-wheels – No single word of this
is any more than decoration of an old self-magnifying wish
to throw the self away so violently and widely that interrogation
has to pause since its chief suspect's sloped off to be cloud, to be
wavery colour bands: no 'release from service to a hard master'
said of the thankful close, it's hoped, of sexual need in oldest age
can touch this other drive of shame fighting to clear a name to itself:
it can't, because its motor runs on a conviction that if I understood
my own extent of blame then that would prove me agent; it doesn't
want to face a likely truth of helplessness – that the inflated will to
gauge and skewer each wrong turn may blank out what's far worse
to bear: impersonal hazard, the humiliating lack of much control –
I don't get past this thought with any confidence.

viii

Thickened with books again, vexed by the
grave again, falling downstairs and not looking

and going outside again there's
a world, there's one in here also

Stay at once in both of them
though not for keeps yet certainly

Then past the quiffs of little trees along the motorway
the streaming lines of ragwort flags
their stuttering yellow
drive my car if I had one
but do keep me company

From PENGUIN MODERN POETS VOL 10 (1996)
and uncollected poems

The Castalian Spring

1

A gush of water, welling from some cave, which slopped
Down to a stone trough squatting stout and chalky as a
Morning sky: I plumped myself on lizard-ridden stone to stare
Into its old truth square that struck me as perhaps another lie
So serious did it look while it promised me, oh, everything.
That honest look of water nursed in stone excited me. Under
The generous trees, tall splotchy planes and brittle ilex, their
Dark flopped down, sun-glare and dust spun through it.

2

I sipped that cold and leafy water tentatively, lost lipstick
Dabbing my mouth, gulped down a little slippery grit I hoped
Was not ferny mosquito larvae; then sat on, guidebook-learned
To get gorgeous and pneumatic in the throat, my bulk deflating
Slowly until the sunset, when the last coach parties slid away.
The heat of the day peeled off, the light got blurred and hummed,
Pounding dusk struck up then a strong swelling rose in my throat
Thick with significant utterance. So, shivery in my cool and newly
Warty skin, I raised this novel voice to honk and boom.

3

I was small enough now, and stoical, to squat on the slabs of rock
Edging the trough, splashed with the spring that welled steadily into it
Shaking its stone-cupped water. I wear yet a precious jewel in my head,
I mused, this line of old rhetoric floating back through me, as quite
Unsurprised I settled to study the night, flexing my long damp thighs
Now as studded and ridged as the best dill pickles in Whitechapel.
Into the cooling air I gave tongue, my ears blurred with the lyre
Of my larynx, its vibrato reverberant into the struck-dumb dusk.

4

What should I sing out on this gratuitous new instrument?
Not much liking minimalism, I tried out some Messiaen,
Found I was a natural as a bassoon, indeed the ondes martenot
Simply oozed out of me. Or should lyric well up less, be bonier?
So I fluted like HD's muse in spiky girlish hellenics, slimmed
My voice down to twig-size, so shooting out stiffly it quivered
In firework bursts of sharp flowers. Or had I a responsibility to
Speak to society: though how could it hear me? It lay in its hotels.

5

I spun out some long lines, let them loop in sound ribbons
Lassoo'ed the high branches where they dangled and trailed
Landing like leathery bats in vacancy – alighted, they pleated,
Composed themselves flawlessly, as lifeless as gloves.

The silence that hung on these sounds made me sheepish.
I fished for my German, broke out into lieder, rhymed
Sieg with *Krieg*, so explaining our century; I was hooked
On my theory of militarism as stemming from lyricism.

6

I'd crouched close by a cemetery; at twilight its keeper
Lit oil lamps in shrines on the pale marble graves, each
Brandishing silver-framed photographs; fresh flowers
For the well-furnished dead shone out amiably, while
The scops owl in residence served up its decorous gulps.
Lights burned on steadfastly in this town of the dead,
Each soul in for a long night, their curtains undrawn.
My monotone croaking rang crude in such company.

7

Black plane trees bent over me, crouched in the night breeze.
For hours I called out on a sonorous roll, growing somewhat self-
Conscious I'd nothing to do but to sound: yet sound was so stirring
And beauty of utterance was surely enough, I thought I had read this.
A wind rose as I tore out my ravishing tenor, or sank down to throb
On my pitted hindquarters while my neck with its primrose striations
Pulsated and gleamed. Then beauty sobbed back to me, shocking,
Its counterpoint catching my harmonies; I had heard a fresh voice.

8

No longer alone, not espousing Narcissus, I answered each peal
In a drum of delirium, recalling with shame the dry white thighs
Of frogs like baked chicken wishbones, sorely in need of a sauce.
Our calls clasped in common, as heavy as love, and convulsively
Thickened by love – until ashamed of such ordinariness, I wailed
In sheer vowels. *Aaghoooh*, I sloughed off *raark, aaarrgh* noises,
Deliberately degenerate; exuded *ooeeehaargh-I-oohyuuuh*; then
Randomly honked 'darkling blue of Dimitrios': I had dreamed that.

9

The voice hears itself as it sings to its fellows – must
Thrum in its own ears, like any noise thumping down
Anywhere airwaves must equably fall. I was not that
Narcissus who stared stunned by his handsomeness;
Or I was, but not culpably, since as I sang, so I loved.
In that action of calling hope out, I embodied it, grew
Solemn and swollen ushering in my own utterance.
I rang florid yet grave in my ears, as I had to.

10

Did I need to account for myself as noise-maker?
I had stared in the windows of Clerkenwell clock shops
At dusty brand oils for the watchmakers' trade, made for
Easing the wound spring – some *horo*-prefixed, and so close

To my horror of time ticking by – brown bottles of clock oil
Labelled Horolene, Horotech. Should I wind up my own time,
Chant 'I was dropped on the Borders, a poor scraplet of
Langholm, illegit. and state's burden, lone mother of three'?

11

Could I try on that song of my sociologised self? Its
Long angry flounce, tuned to piping self-sorrow, flopped
Lax in my gullet – 'But we're all *Bufo bufo'*, I sobbed –
Suddenly charmed by community – 'all warty we are'.
Low booms from the blackness welled up like dark liquid
Of 'wart' Ich auf Dich.' One Love was pulsed out from our
Isolate throats, concertina'ed in common; 'Du mit Mir' was
A comforting wheeze of old buffers, all coupled, one breed.

12

But then I heard others, odd pockets of sound; why wouldn't these
Claim me to chant in their choir? As I grew lonelier I got philosophical,
Piped up this line: 'Don't fall for paradox, to lie choked in its coils
While your years sidle by.' Some hooted reproachfully out of the dawn
'Don't *you* stifle *us* with your egotist's narrative or go soft on ''sameness'',
We'll plait our own wildly elaborate patterns' – they bristled like movies
By Kurosawa. By then I'd reflated, abandoned my toadhood, had pulled on
My usual skin like old nylons. I drifted to Delphi, I'd a temple to see.

Curmudgeonly

A partner is a social-democratic thing to have; so much so that you'll come across couples, long
Solidly-married, yet who'll introduce each other as 'my partner', not 'my wife' or 'husband.'
OK, it's sociologically neat, its journalese copes usefully with mass cohabitation
But the spread of the intimate sense of the word puzzles me. Sexually egalitarian in ways –
Assuming nothing *re* the so-called sexual orientation of the partnered ones – it strikes me
As also innocently, blindly, aristocratic. This maybe is my soured reaction; but I only mean
If you've a private contract to describe a person as your partner, junking all the shackles
Of the state, plunged in a glow of free association – that is fine, but don't you then set up
An unintentional excluding coldness to the millions who through bad luck, mismanagement,
    death or desertion, find themselves un-partnered?
Using 'my spouse' or even the sugary 'my lover' does publicly mark the tracks of a willed act,
    it inscribes an emotional history,
Yet neither sound like mundane attributes that anyone socially competent ought to have.

The lack of glamour of the term 'my partner' could suggest that such an undramatic thing
Is got from any supermarket, rather like 'new toothpaste' or 'some string.'
Of course just what to call them makes you slither (like 'the father of my youngest child', 'a person
I once lived with'?) – but I can't warm to this vogue for 'partner', since not to possess something
So sober yet so mildly venturesome, so virtuously *unlicensed* by the state, sounds worse
Than not being trusted in business, not being picked for even the weakest school netball team.
Surely only a passionate attraction should glue people together; yet better speak it in a reserved
Diction of friendship, or of marriage, legal or no, but for every sex – not this twang of cowboys
Hunched over their baked bean cans, keeping out of the prairie wind, and mighty self-conscious:
'Yup. It's lonesome tonight, kinda cold out there. So, Howdy, partner.' – What happened to
Unsettling love? Or to calmly-conducted if unimpassioned marriages, still exuding
Some generosity? Better a cheerful privacy than this partitioning pseudo-public speech
Of two followed by two, neat and wooden as Noah's Ark. I hear a bloodless future come
In which we'll sidle as usual through attachments whose truthful varieties are beaten flat
Under one leaden word; in which, to nick a line from well-married W. H. Auden,
Thousands have lived without love. Not one without partners.

'Affections of the Ear'

Here's the original Narcissus story: The blue nymph Leiriope, called the lily-faced,
Clear blue as any Cretan iris, got the river-god, summer Cephissus, so on the boil
That lapped by his skeins of water, soused in them, spun round, twirled, interlaced
Until made pregnant, she had Narcissus. Stupefied well before he was pulped to oil
What future did he ever really have, with that slight azure mother of his embraced
By slippery Cephissus, insinuating himself everywhere to flatter, linger and coil?
Leiriope chased Teiresias to set him his very first poser: would her boy be effaced
By a rapid death? The seer said No – just as long as he didn't know himself. Recoil
From the goal of self-knowledge! That maxim, chiselled in temple rock, gets erased
By the case of Narcissus who came to know himself to be loved water. Philosophy
Recommends severe self-scrutiny to us, while a blithe self-indifference is disgraced:
Yet for gorgeous Narcissus to know himself was sheer torment, and his catastrophe.

He did know he was beautiful before he ever caught sight of himself in the water.
A youth he didn't want died cursing 'Let him love, too, yet not get what he'll love.'
(I should explain myself, I sound derivative? Because I am, I'm Echo, your reporter.
I'll pick up any sound to flick it back if it's pitched louder than the mutter of a dove.
I am mere derivation, doomed by Mrs Zeus to hang out in this Thespian backwater.)

[118]

He pushed into the surface of the lake; when push had come, as come it will, to shove
Narcissus had to know. Then deathly recognition drew him lamb-like to his slaughter.
His object was no wavering boy beneath the water, he was far more than hand in glove
With what he saw. I know his problem, though at least I do have Iynx, my bird daughter.
To love himself was pain precisely when he came to understand that truth, most bitterly.
I got hurt too, by ox-eyed Hera as they call her although I'd say cow, recumbent above.
For me, Echo, to forcibly repeat others' words is my ear torment, my own catastrophe.

I told stories so Zeus' lovers escaped, under cover of my chatter they'd slip past Hera.
I did things with words until she caught me, to rage 'False fluency, your gossip's untrue:
You've always wanted the last word – see what good it'll do you.' I was right to fear her
For now I have got it. So exiled, I fell for Narcissus. I had no voice to plead so I'd pursue.
He called 'I'd die before I'd give myself to you!' I shrilled 'Give myself to you!' ran nearer.
If he'd cried 'I'd die before I'd fuck you', at least I could have echoed back that 'Fuck you.'
Sorry – I have to bounce back each last phrase. Half-petrified, I voice dead gorges. Dearer
My daughter Iynx, a wryneck, torticollis, twisted neck, barred and secretive as any cuckoo,
A writher in the woods – as a mother I am, and am merely, responsive; still, I keep near her.
My body goes rocky when I hang round Narcissus. Numbed to a trace of ruined articulacy
I mouth words I can't voice; half-turned to stone, am rigid with memory of what I could do.
So for lonely Narcissus fruitlessly knowing himself as his object was torture, a catastrophe.

He saw truth in fluidity, was an offshoot of water; he dreamily propped himself prone
Beside his reflection; the image that shone yet broke at his touch he did not misconstrue.
He lay dumb in the daze of himself by the glaze of the lake with his face set like stone.
If your mother was blue and your father was water, then mightn't you try to be true?
'Only the thinnest liquid film parts us; which is why, unlike most lovers', I heard him groan,
'I long for more distance between us; only then could I start to get near him.' Narcissus knew.
In the end, he was not misled by vanity. He saw it was himself he loved and not his clone:
In just that lay his torture. I've said that as a bulb he got pulped down to oil, mashed to a stew.
Narcissus oil's a narcotic, both stem from the same root *narcos*, numb; the bulb was known
As the botanical root to cure 'affections of the ear.' (I'll need that oil on my tympanum, too,
If thought is truly a bone.) His becoming a herbal remedy concludes Narcissus' biography.
Dying by water in knowing misery, he's recycled as unguent to drop on the sounding tissue
Of sore ears to heal their affections. Affections of the ear, not of the heart, familiar catastrophe.

'Ears are the only orifices that can't be closed' though force may get some others to succumb.
My inward ears will jam wide open to internal words that overlying verbiage can't smother.
Boated over the Styx, Narcissus' shade peered in its black waters just in case his image swum.
Numbed by affection of his heart, now dried he'll cure the ear affections. Son of his lily mother
His beauty drove me deeper into repetition as a sounding-board, a ringing rock, a mere eardrum.
A rhyme rears up before me to insist on how I should repeat a stanza's formal utterance – other

Than this I cannot do, unless my hearers find a way of speaking to me so I don't stay semi-dumb
Or pirouette, a languid Sugarplum. Echo's a trope for lyric poetry's endemic barely hidden bother:
As I am made to parrot others' words so I am forced to form ideas by rhymes, the most humdrum.
All I may say is through constraint, dictation straight from sounds doggedly at work in a strophe.
'To make yourself seen reflects back to you, but to make yourself heard goes out toward another.'
That's all I, Echo, ever do. Occasionally diverting, it stays my passive hell and small catastrophe.

'Outside from the Start'

i

What does the hard look do to what it sees?
Pull beauty out of it, or stare it in? Slippery

heart on legs clops into the boiling swirl as
a pale calm page shoots up, opening rapidly

to say *I know* – something unskinned me, so
now it bites into me – it has skinned me alive,

I get dried from dark red to dark windspun
withered jerky, to shape handy flyports out

of my lattice, or pulled out am membranes
arched bluish, webby, staked out to twang

or am mouthslick of chewed gum, dragged
in a tearing tent, flopped to a raggy soft sag.

Yet none have hard real edges, since each one
is rightly spilled over, from the start of her life.

How long do I pretend to be all of us.
Will you come in out of that air now.

ii

Black shadows, sharp scattered green
sunlit in lime, in acid leaves.

Hot leaves, veined with the sun
draining the watcher's look of all colour

so a dark film moves over her sight.
Then the trees glow with inside light.

Hold to the thought if it can shine
straight through a dream of failed eyes sliding

to the wristwatch's face, wet under its glass
a thickening red meniscus tilting across its dial.

iii

And then my ears get full of someone's teeth again
as someone's tongue

as brown and flexible as a young giraffe's
rasps all round someone else's story –

a glow of light that wavers and collapses
in a *phttt* of forgiving what's indifferent to it:

not the being worked mechanically but the stare
to catch just what it's doing to you –

there's the revulsion point, puffs up a screen
tacks cushiony lips on a face-shaped gap

a-fuzz with a hair corona, its mouth a navel
not quiet, and disappointing as adult chocolate –

I'd rather stalk as upright as a gang of arrows
clattering a trolley down the aisles

though only the breastbone stone
the fair strung weltering

a softening seashore clay
steel-blue with crimps of early history

the piney trees their green afire
a deep light bubbling to grey

long birds honking across
the scrub, the ruffled shore

coral beaks dab at froth
the pinched sedge shirring

unbroken moor, spinney rushes
petticoat brine, bladderwrack-brown

coppice rustlers, always a one to fall
for – Cut it, blank pennywort charm, or

punch of now that rips the tireless air
or gorgeous finger-stroke of grime.

iv

True sweetness must fan out to find its end
but tied off from its object it will swell –

lumping across sterile air it counts itself
lonely and brave. At once it festers. Why shape

these sentiments, prosecution witnesses, in violet
washes of light where rock cascades to water bluer

than powdering hopes of home. A hook's tossed out
across one shoulder to snag on to any tufts of thrift:

Have I spoken only when things have hardened?
But wouldn't the fact of you melt a watch?

Unfurls no father-car umbrella here. No beautiful
fate is sought, nor any cut-out heart renunciation

– if only some Aztec god could get placated! But he don't –
there's just a swollen modesty to champ at its own breast.

High on itself, it sings of its own end, rejoicing
that this cannot come about. Because I am alive here.

v

The muscled waves reared up, and scrupulously
no hints of mock neutrality were lost.

Containment-led indifference, or conspiracy
accounts of generals' pensions, cost

no setback for the partners of democracy
who portioned barnyards out to each *volost*

while florid in the twilight, Nation stood
alight above the low dismembered good.

Rhetorical

To be air or a black streak on air, or be silt.
Be any watery sheen threading brackish, or vein
nets tracked as patted under their skin glaze, running all ways.

Cascade of stubs.
Buttercup metal glow, ruff of dark strawberry tulle
in any vehement colour night you get blown into hundreds.

Is that clear as a glass stem cups its chill in its own throat.
Is it true that candour so tightens the integument of the heart
that quartz needles shower from the cut mouth of the speaker
though the voice opens to fall:

If you can see me, look away
but swallow me into you

And I must trust that need is held in common, as I think it my duty to.
That every down-draught's thick with stiffening feathers
with rustlings from pallor throats
as the air hangs with its free light and its dead weight equally.

Problems of Horror

Boys play and a horse moves through the woods.
Through perfectly heat-sealed lyric, how to breathe?
He has tailored a cadence out of disgust, and spins to see its hang on him;
privately faint at heart he pirouettes, sporting a lapel nausea carnation.
Who shakes her locks, seaweed hissed branching to blood coral
flirty alright, sat under the painterly sky in this flapping landscape.
China blue swollen in a race of high cloud, full woods, blowing fields,
snatched gill smoke, rain slap of running wind.
Stone looks speak *freeze*.
Not, call the sold earth hyacinthine 'to get the measure of the damaged world'.
The new barbarian's charmed sick
with his real sincerity, sluiced in town georgics fluency, solitude skills.
He knows this smooth emulsion is truly-felt revulsion.
He does not mean to be so pure an isolate, his elegance worries him:
Is beauty good, if it's a furious gloss body of disgust, not porous
and not more of a pitted beauty, penetrable, moody?
But Horror gleams 'we're all complicit, all to blame for cruelty', holding aloft
its fine-tuned shock; naming it *political* but sighing *see me, stay for ever*.

Milk Ink

Don't read this as white ink flow, pressed out
Of retractable nipples. No,
Black as his is mine.

Rain-streaked glass, burnt orange cherry leaves, eye drape of sugar pink.
Don't pin me to frou-frou accident
But let me skate – that

This ganglion cluster should have been born with better eyes
More glowingly deer-like – then instead of being horrified might not
One lift its banging head up off the ground and stroke its streaming hair
And, and, and, and never go away.

Don't read his as white ink flow, shot out
Of retractable. No,
Black as this is mine.

Goethe On His Holidays

I and my truthful knapsack will strike out
To backpack through 'this sea-fog snaked on walls,

Wool snagged on slate, lichen-splodged rocks
In spattered chromes, and cadmium flowered gorse' −

But my neat wooden song does yodel so.
There should be a stop put to all yellow talk,

To these artily crafted details to be seen to.
Nursery hatchings, little dulux squares.

A breathy purity I stalk
Of unheld colour, not grouted with dead stuff:

Colour as honesty, shakiness, seduction, sudden fate;
As irrevocable, steadied to humming greys.

There is nowhere further back than pure blue.
Nowhere to come to that aches more than blue aches

For the pompous mechanics of the human heart lack colour
Which lies closer to breathing. Morality of green for

Everyone! I shine in this fresh equality, I figure us all
In our universal study, released from particular griefs

As we are to imagine an absolutely pure red
Like fine carmine suffered to dry on white porcelain.

– To puff away only that tiniest wretched precision!
Then my tufts of hair should halo out in an ice gale –

Red becomes simpler to reach its integrity.
But blue brings a principle of darkness with it.

Sound will spill out toward silence through its twist
Of nostalgia. But colour swells upward like flame.

And I'm crouched gaping with such watering eyes that I'm
Fumbling again for my little book of metaphors

Because that unboundedness drains me. Plotting my
Dash to specifics, I've made a stiff joke of it: When the

Talk turns to colour, every philosopher sees red. Smile, simile!
I took up my rucksack and sprang modestly away to the coast –

'The caravans like blackened teeth
In a wide grin around the bay.

After the plough then sifting down
Gulls in white furrows being sown.

Grinding away on my left hand
I heard the engine of the sea.

Natural history, do me proud
As cover from the self out loud' –

Quite rapidly I'll get so brightly stupid
Bobbing around between abasement and a balloon

Blind in the green afterglow of a crimson dress
Poised by a pale wall then gone on out of the light

But the girl at the inn will fade, however intently I stare.
And I go walking again all over the moors to sob

That she is a long way off, which is where we shall always keep
her.
No *having* suffices the heart, which must keep integrally red.

It Really Is The Heart

The heart does hurt
and that's no metaphor.
It really is
that 'throbbing muscle' you can't say
since that's 'steel comic-sex meat'

but it does hurt
top mid-left under my shirt
with its atrocious beat.

SAY SOMETHING BACK
(2016)

Maybe; maybe not

When I was a child I spoke as a thrush, I
thought as a clod, I understood as a stone,
but when I became a man I put away
plain things for lustrous, yet to this day
squat under hooves for kindness where
fetlocks stream with mud – shall I never
get it clear, down in the soily waters.

A Part Song

i

You principle of song, what are you for now
Perking up under any spasmodic light
To trot out your shadowed warblings?

Mince, slight pillar. And sleek down
Your furriness. Slim as a whippy wire
Shall be your hope, and ultraflexible.

Flap thinly, sheet of beaten tin
That won't affectionately plump up
More cushioned and receptive lays.

But little song, don't so instruct yourself
For none are hanging around to hear you.
They have gone bustling or stumbling well away.

ii

What is the first duty of a mother to a child?
At least to keep the wretched thing alive – Band
Of fierce cicadas, stop this shrilling.

My daughter lightly leaves our house.
The thought rears up: *fix in your mind this*
Maybe final glimpse of her. Yes, lightning could.

I make this note of dread, I register it.
Neither my note nor my critique of it
Will save us one iota. I know it. And.

iii
Maybe a retouched photograph or memory,
This beaming one with his striped snake-belt
And eczema scabs, but either way it's framed,
Glassed in, breathed hard on, and curated.
It's odd how boys live so much in their knees.
Then both of us had nothing. You lacked guile
And were transparent, easy, which felt natural.

iv
Each child gets cannibalised by its years.
It was a man who died, and in him died
The large-eyed boy, then the teen peacock
In the unremarked placid self-devouring
That makes up being alive. But all at once
Those natural overlaps got cut, then shuffled
Tight in a block, their layers patted square.

v

It's late. And it always will be late.
Your small monument's atop its hillock
Set with pennants that slap, slap, over the soil.
Here's a denatured thing, whose one eye rummages
Into the mound, her other eye swivelled straight up:
A short while only, then I come, she carols – but is only
A fat-lot-of-good mother with a pointless alibi: 'I didn't
Know.' Yet might there still be some part for me
To play upon this lovely earth? Say. Or
Say *No,* earth at my inner ear.

vi

A wardrobe gapes, a mourner tries
Her several styles of howling-guise:

You'd rather not, yet you must go
Briskly around on beaming show.

A soft black gown with pearl corsage
Won't assuage your smashed ménage.

It suits you as you are so pale.
Still, do not get that saffron veil.

Your dead don't want you lying flat.
There'll soon be time enough for that.

vii

Oh my dead son you daft bugger
This is one glum mum. Come home I tell you
And end this tasteless melodrama – quit
Playing dead at all, by now it's well beyond
A joke, but your humour never got cruel
Like this. Give over, you indifferent lad,
Take pity on your two bruised sisters. For
Didn't we love you. As we do. But by now
We're bored with our unproductive love,
And infinitely more bored by your staying dead
Which can hardly interest you much, either.

viii

Here I sit poleaxed, stunned by your vanishing
As you practise your charm in the underworld
Airily flirting with Persephone. Not so *hard*
To imagine what her mother *had gone through*
To be ferreting around those dark sweet halls.

ix

They'd sworn to stay for ever but they went
Or else I went – then concentrated hard
On the puzzle of what it ever truly *meant*
For someone to be here then, just like that,
To not. Training in mild loss was useless
Given the final thing. And me lamentably
Slow to 'take it in' – far better toss it out,
How should I take in such a bad idea. No,
I'll stick it out instead for presence. If my
Exquisite hope can wrench you right back
Here, resigned boy, do let it as I'm waiting.

x

I can't get sold on reincarnating you
As those bloody 'gentle showers of rain'
Or in 'fields of ripening grain' – oooh
Anodyne – nor yet on shadowing you
In the hope of eventually pinpointing
You bemused among the *flocking souls*
Clustered like bats, as all thronged gibbering
Dusk-veiled – nor in modern creepiness.
Lighthearted presence, be bodied forth
Straightforwardly. Lounge again under
The sturdy sun you'd loved to bake in.
Even ten seconds' worth of a sighting
Of you would help me get through
This better. With a camera running.

xi

Ardent bee, still you go blundering
With downy saddlebags stuffed tight
All over the fuchsia's drop earrings.
I'll cry 'Oh bee!' to you, instead –
Since my own dead, apostrophised,
Keep mute as this clear garnet glaze
You're bumping into. Blind diligence,
Bee, or idiocy – this banging on and on
Against such shiny crimson unresponse.

xii

Outgoing soul, I try to catch
You calling over the distances
Though your voice is echoey,

Maybe tuned out by the noise
Rolling through me – or is it
You orchestrating that now,

Who'd laugh at the thought
Of me being sung in by you
And being kindly dictated to.

It's not like hearing you live was.
It is what you're saying in me
Of what is left, gaily affirming.

xiii

Flat on a cliff I inch toward its edge
Then scrutinise the chopped-up sea
Where gannets' ivory helmet skulls
Crash down in tiny plumes of white
To vivify the languid afternoon –
Pressed round my fingertips are spikes
And papery calyx frills of fading thrift
That men call sea pinks – so I can take
A studied joy in natural separateness.
And I shan't fabricate some nodding:
'She's off again somewhere, a good sign.
By now, she must have got over it.'

xiv

Dun blur of this evening's lurch to
Eventual navy night. Yet another
Night, day, night, over and over.
I so want to join you.

xv

The flaws in suicide are clear
Apart from causing bother
To those alive who hold us dear
We could miss one another
We might be trapped eternally
Oblivious to each other
One crying *Where are you, my child*
The other calling *Mother.*

xvi

Dead, keep me company
That sears like titanium
Compacted in the pale
Blaze of living on alone.

xvii

Suspended in unsparing light
The sloping gull arrests its curl
The glassy sea is hardened waves
Its waters lean through shining air
Yet never crash but hold their arc
Hung rigidly in glaucous ropes
Muscled and gleaming. All that
Should flow is sealed, is poised
In implacable stillness. Joined in
Non-time and halted in free fall.

xviii

It's all a resurrection song.
Would it ever be got right
The dead could rush home
Keen to press their chinos.

xix

She do the bereaved in different voices
For the point of this address is to prod
And shepherd you back within range
Of my strained ears; extort your reply
By finding any device to hack through
The thickening shades to you, you now
Strangely unresponsive son, who were
Such reliably kind and easy company,
Won't you be summoned up once more
By my prancing and writhing in a dozen
Mawkish modes of reedy piping to you
– Still no? Then let me rest, my dear.

xx

My sisters and my mother,
Weep dark tears for me
I drift as lightest ashes
Under a southern sea

O let me be, my mother
In no unquiet grave
My bone-dust is faint coral
Under the fretful wave

Four blindfolded songs

The hart he's on the hill.
The stout woodpigeon
Sobs her patient measure
From out a muffled shrub.

How neat her gilded eye
Too spare for garlanded
Ornament. Still to be
Marquetry, and to coo.

*

Past avenues of pines
I'll journey to whiteness.
Small wife at the gate
Be mild as is your nature.

Over bristling plains
By six municipalities
Eagerly I'll bounce
Into a thronged arcade,

Lanterns rosy at night
Looped from mossy tiles.
Rounded in lamplight
Thou, gleaming myriad.

*

Dogged brute paddles
To raise its decent *Arf*
Tail streams feathered
And muzzle jutted out.

Bright brown the water
And bright brown the fur
Near drowned the barking
Through coffee liqueur.

*

Glossed ilex, and the olive groves striped
By dry runnels. Resistible. Went wandering
Up and down & all throughout the town
Past its 'spandrels representing the electric
Telegraph'. There may be a tale, though
A song precede it. That woodpigeon
Groans nicely to fan her leaves, yet not to
Keen, though interlaced with briars, though
We think as our lives have led us to think
Or on the whole; though the dusk settles in
Like . . . like a metaphor. Though *though*.

Tree seen from bed

The fuller leaves are ridged, the newer red.
Sunshine is pooled over them, like lacquer.
One branch catches a notion of movement,
shivering, then the rest cotton on in a rush
roused by the wind, to thrash and vacillate.
A toss-up, where they'll all go next – to lash
around through summer until autumn, that
is where; to fall. May it be managed lightly
though it could well turn wilder beforehand.
Tree watched from my sickbed, read to me.
Read from the hymnal of frank life – of how
to be old, yet never rehearse that fact cosily.

There aren't any stories

Once their stories start up, you'll fall silent —
having no family, can offer them nothing,
can't be one for nostalgia, born illegitimate
in those postwar years when it still counted
as seriously shaming — to some, that shame
should be seared onto their child, much as
paper in sunlight, once rays through a lens
are focused hard onto it, can get blackened
and curl up; now attending wholeheartedly
to the others' old anecdotes, you have none
of your own to trade back; there's not much
to tell about having grown up with hatred.
Nor would you want to get branded again,
for those to whom violence was done aren't
fated to hand it down — it's the doctrinaire
sheltered judge who'll insist everyone must;
you grasped that it burned itself out on you.

Late March

Wry day. Winter, of you
we've had enough. And I have
had enough of sniping memory
or strappy agapanthus leaves in sleet
gone orange at their tips, weak leather.
This charged air has a keen and whitish feel
that stings a little, but has gaiety. So, human you,
I'll hand you back to your own camouflage.
Not as 'bleak weather', though. You might.

Pythian

What, put out on the motorway, will lumber twinkling across the lanes of hazard.

The dog's lovability might rub off on it, when it hides in the straw of his kennel.

Sugared the hillocks of retrospective innocence, while acrid the sheer accidents

of a life, or were they. They were. Now yelps ricochet from a monolith, sat deaf

as is true to its nature. It's got nothing for which to atone, it's the very end stone

in a long row of such silences. For 'a wounded spirit who can bear'— *tell* me. If

it *is* through finding your listener that you'd come to grasp your own monologue, where next could this call turn, massing and purpling as low thunder, though just

whiny to stopped ears; would its *heu* not sink to *phew*, once its weepier appeals tail

off into sepia? No, they'll smoke and foam to whip up a god, or some secular god

who'd be kind to a damp petitioner, but how's her or his correct name made flesh.

Speech-sounds descend, snag in the hair, then flap off to mouth their apostrophes.

A cry reels around, though it's not a Cassandra's but something more speaker-free.

There was and there is a life, I swim in it, but I wouldn't say that it's exactly 'mine'.

Clemency

Sweet goose, fat on spring's
fine ideals, hiss in a lime sauce –

clemency's glow is rueful, citrine-
veined, then always ends up being

about practical kindness – don't tut!
That's brilliantly green and airy

& will frogmarch some right round
under the blinking sun so look lively.

In Nice

Where did they get to?
It's untidy without them;
chic or fanned flat, those
house sparrows in teams.
– Pip, sirrah, southbound
to red dust scuffles. To
where the lemon trees.

Still

You're dead but you still flicker bluish – I'd not
want to jinx anyone by bobbing like you do
right in my eye's corner, it's maddening.
Rather turn stolid, go blocky, be granite, not
whirr and not flare but lodge stock-still, a slab.
Not become fish, or a sea, nothing fluid, no darting,
no welling up after my death in the mouths of the living,
those very few concerned. What they'll make of this
coming great lump of myself, who knows, though
let them be easy. Let it keep inert. But may they
bear it untroubled if despite its stone density
something self-driven that no-one could plan for
or fashion or help or screen out or subdue
still puts up its fight to stay animate.

Composed underneath Westminster Bridge

Broad gravel barges shove the drift. Each wake
Thwacks the stone steps. A rearing tugboat streaked
Past moorhens dabbing floss, spun pinkish-beaked.
Peanuts in caramelised burnt chocolate bake
Through syrupy air. Above, fried onions cake.
Pigeons on steeleyed dates neck-wrestled, piqued,
Oblivious to their squabs that whined and squeaked
In iron-ringed nests, nursed in high struts. Opaque
Brown particles swarm churning through the tide.
That navy hoop of cormorant can compose
A counter to this shield – eagles splayed wide,
Gold martlets – on the bridge's side; it glows
While through the eau-de-nil flaked arches slide
The boats 'Bert Prior' and 'The Eleanor Rose'.

Under the answering sky

I can manage being alone,
can pace out convivial hope
across my managing ground.
Someone might call, later.

What do the dead make of us
that we'd flay ourselves trying
to hear them though they may
sigh at such close loneliness.

I would catch, not my echo,
but their guarantee that this
bright flat blue is a mouth
of the world speaking back.

There is no depth to that blue.
It won't 'bring the principle
of darkness with it', but hums
in repose, as radiant static.

'When we cry to Thee'

Stout voyager, put out
to a black sea. I had no
mother, yet still I have
become one. Marine.
I'm sick inside this single
darkness. Inky swell,
carry me. Hymns ancient
& modern, buoy us up
though I am faithless.

'The eclipse'

Acacias domed by a quick breeze into
shivery plumes, bunched then sinking.
Dusk, crossroads, walker, flats, night.
That rapid wordless halt bewilders me.
Now evening will hold still for years.
Fear has clamped on its stiffened face.
It knows what should have been done.
It understood what it turned away from.

A baptism

Lit as near secular,
blackened in filaments,
violet whips up its
rich voices into airily
massed *ah oh ah ohs*
as it stings in divining
some men clumped in
pale muslin by water a
washier blue than the sky
clean as its lanky dove.

Silent did depart

'A spirit casts no shadow' – true, of the filmy dead.
Not of a living creature tapering itself to an obelisk.
Rocky mute, life's too serious for this not speaking!
Don't be stuccoed so hard over any humane seepage.

What had been churning round in that ardent pillar?
You'd not have dreamed an upright man could petrify.
Drape my anointing hair at the feet of superb cement.
All hindsight shakes itself out vigorously like a wet dog.

With Child in mind

And when he came to the
broad river, he took off
his coat and swam. There
were reed beds, whistling.

Smoke. Burning somewhere
on the rainy wind, far
along the sobbing wind.
Get away with you now.

Krasnoye Selo

Below a charcoal sky
leaching the squat houses,
days tighten round each
other as the hours weaken.

Umbrellas and their carriers
go slipping to their tasks.
By dusk they've quickly
dwindled away, got tiny.

Shoes sound so pointed
on their way to nowhere.
Purposefully they'll clop
through the constricted air.

Moving toward my silence
I'll speak evening thoughts
sparkling with reproach though
I had meant to forgive.

Listening for lost people

Still looking for lost people – look unrelentingly.
'They died' is not an utterance in the syntax of life
where they belonged, no *belong* – reanimate them
not minding if the still living turn away, casually.
Winds ruck up its skin so the sea tilts from red-blue
to blue-red: into the puckering water go his ashes
who was steadier than these elements. Thickness
of some surviving thing that sits there, bland. Its
owner's gone nor does the idiot howl – while I'm
unquiet as a talkative ear. Spring heat, a cherry
tree's fresh bronze leaves fan out and gleam – to
converse with shades, yourself become a shadow.
The souls of the dead are the spirit of language:
you hear them alight inside that spoken thought.

After 'Nous n'irons plus au bois'

We've had it with the woods.
The underbrush got felled.
Grab who you want, now
that there's no more cover.
None left for a cicada. Do
we let that beauty leap and
see her thump the ground
we'd cleared of dying laurel?
Sweet-throated warbler, yelp.
Off trots the she-shepherd
with a basket for briar roses
or strawberries, should the
churned earth house them.

Orphic

I've lived here dead for decades — now you
pitch up gaily among us shades, with your
freshly dead face all lit up, beaming — but
after my long years without you, don't think
it will be easy. It's we dead who should run
whispering at the heels of the living, yet you,
you'd put the frighteners on me, ruining
the remains of your looks in bewailing me,
not handling your own last days with spirit.
Next you'll expect me to take you around
introducing some starry goners. So mother
do me proud and hold your white head high.
On earth you tried, try once again in Hades.

'I told it not'

Tap, in this bland October
that cedar's ripening cones
piped pinkish green along
its lower branches, tap until
their pollen spills to writhe
in bright lime powder coils.
This frankly panto jealousy
makes it such a lurid tree.

Following Heine

I cried in my sleep as I thought
you were in your grave, I woke but
went on weeping. I dreamt you'd
abandoned me, I woke to cry bitterly.
I slept. In my sleep, I wept as I
dreamt you were still good to me.
I awoke in unrelenting tears.

And another thing

Some new arrival's coming, whose name may not be happy.
Attend it. Childishly lovely, once, to listen to anyone new
as if even the oldest harm was outgrown as a liberty bodice.
Does sifting through damage ease, or enshrine it; how grasp
a past, but not skid on embittered accounting? The ledgers
exhibit their black surplus malice and red lack of tenderness,
while 'suffering' easily gets competitive as each suspects hers
was the rougher lot, yet feels shy out of shame at her history
that won't dovetail with her present. Hoist personalised flags
though they're so stiff with encrusted blood they'd first need
a good sousing in tears? – forget that. Could the years have
been easier if you'd just settled early on hating a sex instead,
although which one of them to begin with? Sleeked up your
plumes to swan out and ruffle your usual vexers of dailiness?
Filed reports to the muses, via cicadas' surveillance, on men
who weren't rapt, only dozing in warm grass at noon, lulled
by music to dreaming their sonic enchantment is virtuously
militant, a sparkly art stance plus a strong civic end in itself?
It's late. 'You must live as you can', which is all we ever did.

Boxy piece

Exhibit of small boxes made from wood
to house their thought and each an open
coffin of the not-dead with their chirring.
Satin-lined frames stack square in blocks
nested to a columbarium – then mumble,
closet doves, whose fond carpenter drills
piercings for more air, won't let you flap.

Catastrophic thinking

It willed to be ordinary, easy
as rain sifting through woods
but doubt shrouded that mind
skewing its aim at mildness.

Fires were lit and sap hissed
in young branches torn down
by anxiety contorted to shield
itself, biting its angry hands.

It smoked out each transparent joy.
It strode well away from its heart.
Darkness absorbs any mind, once
it starts calling itself 'unwanted'.

The patient who had no insides

i The ins and outs of it

As clouds swell to damply fill gaps in mountains, so in
Illness we sense, solidly, our entrails expanding to stuff
That space of our innerness just feebly imagined before.

I'd slumped at home before the nightly documentaries
Of scalpels nipping through the primrose fat, beaded
With that orange hue that blood becomes on camera,

But only when they crossly assert themselves do those
Guts I hadn't believed in, truly come home in me.
Figuratively, yes, we've guts – literally, may suspect

We haven't – poking sceptical as Doubting Thomases
For what's packed below skin we don't see laid bare.
Invaginated folds, ballooning orifices, we know about

And pregnancy, watching some unborn other's heels
Nudging and butting like carp snouts under the navel.
That's someone else altogether, palpable inside me.

No, it's my disbelief in my own entrails that I mean.
I'd glimpsed the radiographer's dark film, starring
Barium-whitened swags of colon, mine. Blown glass,

Hooped entrails ridged with their glazed diverticules
Like little suckers studded plumply on squid tentacles
Of my intestines. But now I see their outer evidence:

My ginger skin. How well you look, they'd said to me
At work. But no tan browned my face. The malady
Conveyed an air of robust health through bronzing me.

ii On the ward of signs and humours

Now foamy bracken-brown urine cools in plastic jugs
For measuring on the ward, frothed like a hillside stream
Relaxing into pools. 'What says the doctor to my water?'

Jaundice is read as if the humours still remained reliable.
There were insides inside me – now they've gone all wrong.
Modern regimes of signs set in, and newly prudent thoughts

That what they stamp, we own. Pointers to a depth, to be
'Philosophically, Medicinally, Historically open'd & cut up'.
From Burton's ripe account of melancholy, that last quote.

The sorrows brood inside our purplish spleens, barriers
That check dark moods of sultry bile by segregating it
Where it can't seep to hurt us. Anatomised emotion.

'Pancreas' means 'all flesh'. Now, awry, it chews itself.
That piece of ambient meat I am eats meaty me all up.
Enzymes flood to champ their host, their prey – that's

Me. They don't know where to stop. I'm auto-gesting.
Spontaneous combustion in a schlock Victorian engraving
Of hearthrug scorched, charred ankles jutting out of boots,

No more of faithful Lizzie left. A hapless autophage I am
Whose fizzog has gone bad. Enzymes digesting tissue grind
In rampant amylase and swollen lipase counts. Sure signs

Affecting the liver, a plush nursery for the vegetal spirit.
Fondly this warming organ clasps the stomach set over it
Fingering heat into it, nursing its charge, so Galen held.

Flame-like, this liver, slow-cooking the stomach's stuff
Down to a bloodlike juice. Not boiling it dry to char it
Or simmering it to gruel – if the liver's temper is right.

Noble the strong liver, 'dark monarch' to Neruda.
But ignoble, the long slim pear of the gall bladder
And the sole-like spleen, roughened, its shoe shape

Splayed into an ox tongue. Spleen, milky-pulped
Innocent home to the darkest of humours, frees all
Merriment in its bearer, by holding black bile apart

And so, wrote Harvey, 'the spleen causes one to laugh'.
Dreaming of red things, the sanguine man keeps bluff,
Night dreads held safely at bay. Splenetic laughter!

'Remembering mine affliction and my misery
The wormwood and the gall.' So cries Lamentations
Too harsh on the house of that yellow emulsifier,

Hard too on wormwood – a friend, boiled to absinthe,
To smoky Verlaine, and the maker of Pernod's fortune.
Antique are that shrubby vermifuge's properties: bitter

Carminative, anthelmintic, cholagogue, febrifuge,
Swelling the secretion of both liver and gall bladder.
Bluish or red-brown skin markings today? Bad signs.

iii The patient longs to know

Back on the ward, the darting housemen, veering,
Swerve low by ends of beds like swifts, but then zoom off.
Come back! the impatient patient wails, though silently,

Why am I 'nil by mouth' for endless days? Am I each day
Prepped for some other op which never comes – or what?
Unreadable as a leaving lover, no houseman stops to say.

'Your notes got lost so we might send you back, pre-op.
Without your write-up, no, the anaesthetist won't like it.'
My starved heart sinks at hearing this; it's bodily starved

Like all the rest of me, so long on 'nil by mouth'. Nil
In my own mouth, yes, to eat or drink – but also nil
Issued as word of explanation from a doctor's mouth.

Let me go home so I can find things out. Googling
Fulfils the nineteenth century's dream of ardent enquiry
Amassed, and nearly democratically. On medics' sites

The grand Miltonic phrases of the biliary tract race home:
Islets of Langerhans, Ampulla of Vater, Duct of Santorini,
Sphincter of Oddi. Sonorous names, some the narrowings

Which, blocked, can cause grave trouble. They had for me;
That gall bladder, choked, must go. But will its ghost
Kick up in me, once it is tossed away? This oddness of

Owning spare parts. Our bodies littered with redundancies,
Walking reliquaries rattling our appendices, blunt tails,
Primordial. For we are birds with teeth and empty crops.

iv The consultant summarises our national health

'Liver, until so recently the Cinderella of medicine!
Just the girl in the clinical ashes, unrescued as yet
Assailed by her bad suitors – weak policies and folly.

'Alcohol-led liver failure rising, bile duct cancer rates
Mounting, more cirrhosis from viral illness, Hep B, C.
More drinking, younger drinking, increased steatosis,

'Yet funders don't cough up for self-induced sickness.
Specialists get scarcer, beds vanish, bureaucracy swells
As need begs for new transplants, more artificial livers.

'One gets despondent. Lifestyle's the problem,' adds
This eminent hepatologist, despondent at 'patching up
Self-harming patients, worsened by government policy'.

His time is short. This patient nods and leaves. So
It's our national fantasy, not just my private idiocy,
That what our daily intake is by mouth has nil effect?

v Discharged

'Your liver tests are squiffy, Mrs R, but you might
As well go home, you won't get well in here' — then
He's darted off again, mercurial houseman. Outside
The well ones all charge past us like young bullocks,
Amazingly confident. Those who were ill go gingerly.
A smack of post-ward colour shoves us back to life.

Hiding in plain sight

I try to find you, yet you are not here.
I've studied absence, fought to fill it in —
courage comes easier with a grasp of why.

A secret's camouflaged when unconcealed.
I chose to not see/saw the thing too near?
Absence turns thicker, muscled by its strain.

A moon in daylight, whitest blue on blue,
surprises briefly, to appear surreal
until it slips to rights. I couldn't spot

the obvious — *obviam*, in the way; plain
sight goes blind through chasing clarity.
I looked for you, so couldn't see you gone.

I sensed your not-there in its burning life.
I listened out to feel its silence beat.
It does not speak with any human mouth.

Lines starting with La Rochefoucauld

'It is more shameful to distrust your friends
than be deceived by them': things in themselves
do hold – a pot, a jug, a jar, Sweet Williams'
greenshank shins – so that your eye's pulled
clear of metallic thought by the light constancy
of things, that rest there with you. Or without.
That gaily deadpan candour draws you on.
Your will to hope quickens in their muteness.

Oh go away for now

Persistent are your lost or dead
intimates and buried child.

They won't leave their wants unsaid
but tag you with appeals and prods

while your 'work of mourning' quails
before each sibilant attack

inveigling you to lead them back:
'You've loved us terribly, and so

you've kept us going, even though . . .'
Calmly heap fresh soil upon them.

They can wait for you to join them
as soon you will; you'll soon gang up

to poke and give some new grief to
whoever, left living, once loved you.

On the Black Isle

Three ginger temples of oil rigs clamped at the bay's mouth, a
big navy sky roiled over cloud pillars; the notebook goes riffling
through its colour chart for rose-flushed stonework cut clean as
these rain-beaded fuchsias or until that notebook, a mental one,
flips round to enquire whitely: *Just what do you think you're up to?*
'Any gay thing's worth a chase, for as long as its shade distracts –
so drape, far rain, hung in cinematic swathes.' Its next reproach
isn't appealing, either: *So where am I in this?* 'We aren't – this is in
rosy Cromarty, its broad fields racing by and silvery ruthless rain
nettling our scoured skins.' – Quite vanished, and never said why.
Thick kelp straps gleam in the shallows and loll on the rising tide.

'They saw you coming'

I don't resemble my face.
Once it had looked like me.
Who'd have seriously thought
Damage would pounce again.
No, nothing ever gets learnt.
Some slaps and yet another
Bright blind sunshiny day.
Maybe that's as well, since
Experience deduces in tears
The odds-on return of harm.
Better then not to study
Its adamant heartsick brief.

A man 'was stood' there

On pitted sand the urchin shards fan out, but the watcher's
braced in shingle, wet grit scraping around ankles rammed
in an undertow, wrack fronds whipped on skin as he senses
himself raced faster than pebbles grinding toward the rising
water, while his feet stream out behind him in a moonwalk.
You'd get rushed backwards just by standing still, he'll muse
catching a tiniest roaring underfoot – but what thought does
he find in that sound, or purely his dizziness on being rolled
away from the sea, as one lost to his naturally rocky balance
that he'll recalibrate now at the core of a man 'being stood'.

Percy's Relique;
on the Death of John Hall's Peacock

Earl Percy of Brook Mill, in gown
Of brown with azure trimmings, flown!

Grand and admired fowl, indenturing
John your janitor to toss you copious nuts,

Rare! Raoaark! Rare! You were adornment.
You were Brook Mill. Its visitors were yours.

You Shelley to us duller poets, Percy. Flare!
Go, glittering! Your fan recalls you from her desk

Lamenting, where our London peafowls droop
And sigh for iridescent Percy and his shrieks.

An awkward lyric

It sits with itself in its arms. Out of
the depth of its shame it starts singing
a hymn of pure shame, surging in the throat.
To hold a true note could be everything.
Getting the hang of itself would undo it.

Cardiomyopathy

Unlovely meaty thing, a heart – unlikeliest
'seat of the affections'. Indifferent to its human
wrapper, the brute pigheaded muscle wallops on.
It is a pump, impersonal in its lub-dup shunt.
But it can be a pump that stops itself, if its cells
have grown awry, like toppled pancakes; that
kind of heart will get too big for its own good.
Self-sabotage, on auto-pilot, starts to fatten it.
Its septum thickens silently as the thing slogs on
about its idiot work of self-enlargement, or until
its motor limps and a surprise arrhythmia makes
it choke and stagger like a flooding carburettor
while its electrics race, then quiver, then go still.
I've had to work this out alone. I'm sounding
too forensic? – but you'll go on with your dead,
go as far as you can; that's why my imagination
wouldn't wait outside the morgue, but burst in
to half-anaesthetise itself with knowing; as I was
the witness to his start as an ivory and ice-blue
newborn cyanosed by my long labour, sliced out
by caesarean, so I did try to keep him company
even after the end, when his too-big heart got
flopped down on a metal tray to bare the weak
fold in its mitral valve, and the glossy cling-film
of lilac membranes coating its large ventricles –
I can't quite leave the autopsy room for good.

My living on indicts me. If my own heart
contracted briefly, it still pushed on past yours.

Hearts, being muscular, power on as they can.
Mine was relentless in outpacing yours.

'The heart is a hard flesh, not easily injured'
so Galen wrote. He bypassed those like yours.

My heart, though old, seems tough enough and so
I would have gladly had it changed, for yours.

There is heart failure, and however well we mean,
the failure's mutual; though the worse loss is yours.

Touristic in Kyoto

Irises, by a pond freckled with spring waterweed.
Hiding from the wind, an onlooker dabs away
to get herself clean out of the picture,
leaving no colour note.
Better, no picture – certainly
no 'thin rain of blossom'.

Little Eva

Time took your love – now time will take its time.
'Move on', you hear, but to what howling emptiness?
The kinder place is closest to your dead
where you lounge in confident no-motion, no thought
of budging. Constant in analytic sorrow, you abide.
It even makes you happy when you're feeling blue.
Jump up, jump back. Flail on the spot.
I can disprove this 'moving-on' nostrum.
Do the loco-motion in my living room.

*This poem contains brief excerpts from the lyrics to
'The Loco-Motion', words and music by Gerry Goffin and Carole
King, originally performed by Eva Boyd as Little Eva.*

Never to disinter the pink companion

Never to disinter the pink companion. Wintry. So isn't everyone
drawn to human warmth, if only by animal curiosity? Seems not.
Then how pleasantly to give back his enigma of wordless absence
to its real owner, like a jacket he'd not realised he'd left behind?
Worse, he had: 'Thanks a lot for another trip to the charity shop.'
To confess my bafflement with grace. So, tolerant Grace, though
I've needed to call for you so often, please don't ignore my knocks
but uncoil from your couch and ease out of your door, smiling, to
me mulish with a little scar literature, it is a very late form of love.

Let no air now be sung

Let no air now be sung, let no kind air —
sorrow alone reveals a constant pulse.
A trusted oak deceives the pliant back
coiled into it like a fern shoot aping an
archbishop's crook held high as a truth
paraded through hazy woods in its veil
to get snapped off by that wild anxiety
figuring its jail could be quit in a slash
clean down to her dear bone — it wills
to twitch its hem aside and motor on.
Let no air now be sung, let no kind air.

'I admit the briar'

I admit the briar.
The grave rose knots it,
both wound about in shade.

A padded heart draws barbs —
worked free, they won't make
relics however buffed up.

Full of wist, I needn't be.
The fuller world's not 'cruel' to me
more like indifferent —

I am that world. What was it
Flora Tristan cried
in her corkscrew gaiety:

'When I behold Thy crown of thorns,
Thy bitter trials, O Lord, how trivial
do they seem compared to mine!'

You men who go in living flesh

You men who go in living flesh
Scour clean then drape your souls
In plumy dress that they may rise
Clear of those thrashing shoals

Of mackerel of the sea who call
You loiterers on the strand
To heed your future salted lungs
Pegged out to dry on sand.

I was upright upon the field
Another thing in the sea.
Its light has washed my eyelids shut.
Green grass floats over me.

Hope is an inconsistent joy
Yet blazes to renew
Its lambent resurrections of
Those gone ahead of you.

Death makes dead metaphor revive

Death makes dead metaphor revive,
Turn stiffly bright and strong.
Time that is felt as 'stopped' will freeze
Its to-fro, fro-to song

I parrot under feldspar rock
Sunk into chambered ice.
Language, the spirit of the dead,
May mouth each utterance twice.

Spirit as echo clowns around
In punning repartee
Since each word overhears itself
Laid bare, clairaudiently.

An orphic engine revs but floods
Choked on its ardent weight.
Disjointed anthems dip and bob
Down time's defrosted spate.

Over its pools of greeny melt
The rearing ice will tilt.
To make *rhyme* chime again with *time*
I sound a curious lilt.

'A gramophone on the subject'

1 The postwar exhumation squad's verses

Exhumation squads dug to unearth them
In bits that got dropped in cloth bags
While one man stood by with his notebook
Recording all readable tags.

It was not the most popular service
Retracing those old trench charts
Then shaking off well-rotted khaki
From almost unknowable parts.

One father pitched up to bribe us
To hand him a charred scrap of shirt.
He'd worked out it was his son there.
We told him the thing was just dirt.

Blood mud had thickened to rich mud
Which settled as grassed-over clay.
Matching pieces with names wasn't easy
Despite what 'their' new headstones say.

2 'It isn't catching, you know'

Those of a tender conscience swear
Their vows that they will fail to keep.
At the first whiff of human need
Each scatters like a panicked sheep.

You had believed that some might stay,
So earnestly they'd sworn they would.
Without one word they slipped away
To save themselves – that's understood.

When each in turn gets hit by loss
Who but himself will cluster round.
A black joke – 'mutual empathy' –
To faces set like hardened ground.

3 'If any question why'

We do not draw our curtains closed.
We're told we should not mind
This change from custom; our old way
Would make whole streets look blind.

What all this means may yet come clear.
Telegrams, at more doors, 'regret'.
You can't ask what's the good of it.
Their names might get in the *Gazette*.

4 'Tucked in where they fell'

'Tucked in' is not quite how we'd put it.
We weren't plumped up neatly in bed.
If you 'fell' as one piece you were lucky,
Not dismembered before you were dead.

We wore dog-tags of vulcanised fibre
But those need their dog to stay whole
Or to keep enough bone to be tied on
Not be draped off some tree in a scroll.

Had we managed to get home living
We'd trouble you worse than the dead.
Shambling, like blind men, among you
And most probably gone in the head.

So we've formed our heavenly choir
Composed of our melded limbs.
Each voices his part in the singing.
We can't disentangle our hymns.

We get noisy as larks in the sunshine.
Your leg's with his head over there.
My fist's stuck upright from a dugout
And it's clutching a hank of his hair.

5 'Their Name Liveth For Evermore'

Death's tidied up in rows and lists.
The scratched are 'Known to God'.
'He is not missing: he is here' –
Else in the awkward squad.

His name's got weightier than him.
He's been peeled off from it.
It didn't much suit him in his life.
That went AWOL. Poor fit.

What is it for some name to 'live'?
It's lifeless. Set in stone.
Its bearer proved too slight for it.
He'd always been 'Unknown'.

6 'Death of a Hero'

'I droop', it pales, 'like a solitary wood anemone'.
But they're surrounded by their white-faced friends
and each of them gets wind-whipped – then, solitary
as an unpretty thing lamenting *help me*, if too quietly.
It is the painted mouth gurning behind its bars. Best
if it forgets to be ham, or plant, or to have attributes.

7 'He lies somewhere in France'. Somewhere.

What can it mean, that someone walks
out of your house then they won't come

back ever. When you'd had them, and
they were boys; you'd think they'd make

their own way home out of that mud.
He was like a cat, always fell on his feet.

I can feel he's still working in the fields
or is drinking late somewhere – oh I do

know that he's not & yet none of it fits.
Then what could it mean to *know* this.

We learnt that the line between here
and there is a faint grey, and it gleams

like the honesty's seedpods – as brittle.
But candid somehow. Hard to convey

how it seems fresh, and almost papery.
You could poke a hole and be straight

through onto the death side, where it
is livelier than here, and a lot clearer.

I never could grasp human absence.
It always escaped me, the real name

of this unfathomable simplest thing.
It's his hands I remember the most.

But that'll go. Some women take on
a wary look and seem bleached out.

They get pierced by a casual remark
that makes them harden or go vague.

'I fought for strength and tearlessness
and found both.' What price pride.

No need to draw attention to yourself.
So many were left as quiet as you. Do

I go on for years thinking and thinking.
One in all these thousands. Him. Me.

So many gone that you can't take it in.
Whatever I say is bound to sound flat.

I am a gramophone on the subject.
Each day's same horizon to be faced.

You long to fade out into it, yourself.
I look doggedly after a missing figure.

What to do now is clear, and wordless:
You will bear what can not be borne.

Notes and acknowledgements

From DRY AIR, Virago, 1985

These are versions of poems written between 1796 and 1806 by
Friedrich Hölderlin (1770-1843).

From MOP MOP GEORGETTE, Reality Street Editions, 1993

'Letters from Palmer' draws extensively on *The Letters of Samuel
Palmer* edited by Raymond Lister, Oxford University Press,
1974.

'A shortened set' adapts a line from a traditional song from
Nigeria, and repeats one Stevie Winwood phrase and a Lesley
Gore line from 'It's My Party' written by W. Gold, J. Gluck Jnr.
and H. Wiener. The paintings referred to in 'A shortened set'
are by Ian McKeever.

'Wherever you are, be somewhere else' is a title based on the
Nintendo Game Boy slogan; the italicised phrases in the poem
are adapted from the old Chuvash, from the play *The Peach
Blossom Fan* by K'ung Shang-jen, and from the ballads 'Fair
Annie of Lochryan' and 'Sweet Willie and Fair Annie' in
Alexander Gardner's *The Ballad Minstrelsy of Scotland*, 1893
– also a source of the lines italicised in 'Knowing in the Real
World'.

'*Lure*, 1963' uses the title of a painting by Gillian Ayres. It quotes
or rephrases song lyrics: 'The Great Pretender' written by Buck
Ram, recorded by The Platters, 'The Wanderer' written by
Ernest Maresca, sung by Dion, 'It's In His Kiss' by Rudy Clark,
sung by Betty Everett, and the title of 'When Will I Be Loved',

written by Phil Everly, recorded by The Everly Brothers.

'A misremembered lyric' uses a phrase from 'Rhythm of the
Rain', written by J. Gummoe, sung by The Cascades, and from
'Something's Gotta Hold Of My Heart' by R. Cook and R.
Greenaway, recorded by Gene Pitney; the poem also quotes a
line from Graham Greene's version of a 1930s song.

Marvin Gaye is quoted in 'Shantung'.

The line from God is adapted from Proverbs 27, verse 17.

'Rayon' ends with the line sung by Neil Sedaka.

The first line of 'Marriage song' recalls one by Jon Ward, written
circa 1969.

'Well all right' includes a phrase from 'Life', written by Sylvester
Stewart, recording as Sly Stone.

'Dark Looks' has an italicised borrowing from the script of
Bertrand Blier's *Les Valseuses*, spoken by Jeanne Moreau.

In 'Seven Strangely Exciting Lies', the sub-title 'Take two of these
tablets tonight and in the morning go on living' follows Terence
Rattigan's *The Deep Blue Sea* and 'Lucille's tune' draws on the
refrain in the Penniman/Collins song 'Lucille', covered by The
Everly Brothers. 'Seven Strangely Exciting Lies' takes its title
from W. H. Auden's 'The Question':

'Only remembering the method of remembering
Remembering only in another way
Only the strangely exciting lie'

From PENGUIN MODERN POETS VOL 10

In 'Affections of the Ear', all details of the story of Narcissus and
Echo here are taken straight from Ovid's *Metamorphoses*, Book
III. Robert Graves' first volume of *The Greek Myths* claims that

narcissus oil was used as a cure for 'affections of the ears'. Here the word 'affection' is an archaism for 'disease' (an example from the *OED* –'an affection of the heart' was, in 1853, a heart disease). The poem has resurrected Ovid's anti-hero who *did* realise his mistake of falling in love with his own reflection; so it offers the first Narcissus, well before the concept of narcissism. Lacan's *The Four Fundamental Concepts of Psychoanalysis* contains the line 'In the field of the unconscious the ears are the only orifice that cannot be closed' while 'Making oneself seen comes back to the subject, but making oneself heard goes out towards the other' repeats his extension of Freud there. The poem wonders about these assertions, as it suggests that Echo may be a figure or a trope for the troubled nature of lyric poetry, driven by rhyme, condemned to repetition of the cadences and sound-associations of others' utterances.

The title of 'Outside from the Start' is from Merleau-Ponty, *The Phenomenology of Perception*: 'Nothing determines me from outside, not because nothing acts upon me, but on the contrary because I am from the start outside myself and open to the world.'

In 'Goethe On His Holidays', some phrases translated from Goethe's *Theory of Colour* and from Brusatin's *History of Colour* have been adapted and incorporated.

'The Castalian Spring' and 'Affections of the Ear' also appeared in my *The Words of Selves: Identification, Solidarity, Irony* (Stanford University Press, USA, 2000).

In addition to the collections already cited, some of these poems appeared in *A Calendar of Modern Letters, Active in Airtime, Angel Exhaust, Angle, Comparative Criticism 19, Conductors of Chaos, Critical Quarterly, Equofinality, Exact Change Yearbook,*

Four Falling, Five Fingers Review, fragmente, Garuda, Grille, Infolio, Metre, New American Writing 8 & 9, The New British Poetry, New Orleans Review, Other: British and Irish Poetry Since 1970, Out of Everywhere, PN Review, Parataxis, The Penguin Book of Poetry From Britain and Ireland Since 1945, Poetical Histories 26, Raddle Moon, Scarlet, Stair Spirit, Stand. I am very grateful to the editors of these journals, collections, or anthologies.

From SAY SOMETHING BACK, Picador, 2016

Acknowledgements
Some of these poems first appeared online, or in paper form, in *Blackbox Manifold* [2013]; *Intercapillary Space* [2013, 2014]; *Snow* [2013]; *English* [2015]; *Constitutional Information* [2015]; *Poetry London* [2014]; *Poetry Ireland Review* [2015]; *Earth Has Not Any Thing To Shew More Fair: A Bicentenary Celebration of Wordsworth's 'Sonnet Composed Upon Westminster Bridge'* [The Wordsworth Trust and Shakespeare's Globe, 2002]; *London Review of Books* [2012]; *Signs and Humours: The Poetry of Medicine* [Calouste Gulbenkian Foundation, 2007]; *The Pity* [The Poetry Society, 2014]; *Translation Games* [Arts and Humanities Research Council, 2015]; *Zone* [2013]; *Shearsman 97 & 98* [2013/2014]; *UEA LDC Poetry Reading Series* [Eggbox, 2014], London Review Bookshop Samplers, No. 1: Denise Riley [Face Press, 2018]. I thank all the editors and publishers concerned, including those who commissioned some of this work. The collection's title is taken from W. S. Graham's 'Implements in their Places' in *New Collected Poems: W. S. Graham*, ed. Matthew Francis [Faber and Faber, London, 2004, p.247].

Notes

In 'Four blindfolded songs' the spandrels are by George Frampton,
    on Electra House, 84 Moorgate, London.
'Composed under Westminster Bridge' has in mind Wordsworth's
    'Composed Upon Westminster Bridge'. It was commissioned
    for *Earth Has Not Any Thing To Shew More Fair: A Bicentenary
    Celebration of Wordsworth's 'Sonnet Composed Upon Westminster
    Bridge'*, The Wordsworth Trust and Shakespeare's Globe, 2002.
'The eclipse' follows the closing scene of Michelangelo Antonioni's
    1962 film, *L'Eclisse*.
'A baptism' refers to Piero della Francesca's 'The Baptism of Christ'
    in the National Gallery, London.
'Following Heine' draws on Heinrich Heine's 'Ich hab' im Traum
    geweinet' from his *Lyric Intermezzo*.

Notes to 'The patient who had no insides'

These are taken from my sequence commissioned for *Signs and
    Humours, The Poetry of Medicine*, edited by Lavinia Greenlaw,
    Calouste Gulbenkian Foundation, London 2007. I'm grateful
    to Professor Roger Williams for his observations, relayed in
    section iv.
Falstaff, in *Henry IV, Part 1*, asks 'What says the doctor to my
    water?'
The subtitle of Robert Burton's *Anatomy of Melancholy*, 1621,
    includes 'Philosophically, Medicinally, Historically open'd and
    cut up'.
Galen, c. AD 200, describes the liver as clasping and warming the
    stomach to cook its contents. He held that the gall bladder,
    spleen and liver produced and stored three of the four bodily
    humours; yellow bile, black bile, and sanguine.

Pablo Neruda wrote an 'Ode to the Liver', 1956.

In 1635 William Harvey termed the liver a noble organ, but the spleen ignoble, describing it as like an ox tongue or a sole of a foot.

In Nicholas Culpeper's *Astrological Judgement of Diseases from the Decumbiture of the Sick*, 1655, the sanguine man 'dreameth of red things'.

Wormwood as a remedy for digestive ills included absinthe, which was manufactured by Henri-Louis Pernod in 1797.

The 'bad signs' of rampaging enzymes in severe acute pancreatitis include bluish and reddish-brown skin discoloration.

'Percy's Relique; on the Death of John Hall's Peacock' imitates Wallace Stevens' poem 'Bantams in Pine-Woods'.

'I admit the briar' was commissioned by *Poetry Ireland Review* for the 150th anniversary of Yeats' birth. It begins with the first line of W. B. Yeats' poem 'A First Confession' in his 'A Woman Young and Old'.

Notes to 'A Gramophone on the Subject'

These verses come from my sequence 'A gramophone on the subject' in *The Pity* [The Poetry Society, 2014], commissioned as part of a commemoration in poetry of the 1914–1918 war. They draw on historical records, including soldiers' and civilians' letters, diaries and memoirs.

1 The postwar exhumation squad's verses

Bodies were often destroyed beyond recognition, after repeated bombardment. The 'exhumation squads' were soldiers who

did the work of disinterring already buried remains from the
battlefields, for reburial in the new military cemeteries nearby.
They'd note any intact identification tags. Occasionally some
determined parents would travel to where the exhumation
squads were working and try to get hold of their son's remains to
take home. They were supposed to be stopped from doing this.

2 *'It isn't catching, you know'*
These lines voice the darkly sensitised thoughts of the
contemporary bereaved about the tendency of some to avoid
them. What lasting silences might have set in after 1914–
1918, when thousands had died, but when public religious
commemoration often took the form of respecting their 'national
sacrifice'? In her 'A Sketch of the Past', Virginia Woolf wrote
'That is one of the aspects of death which is left out when
people talk of the message of sorrow: they never mention
its unbecoming side: its legacy of bitterness, bad temper, ill
adjustment.'

3 *'If any question why'*
The wearing of black armbands, the closing of household curtains
after a death, and other mourning rituals were gradually
abandoned after the start of the 1914–1918 war. The *'Gazette'*
is *The London Gazette*, in which details of those who'd been
awarded military service medals were published, often
posthumously. My title comes from Rudyard Kipling's couplet,
'If any question why we died/ Tell them, because our fathers lied.'

4 *'Tucked in where they fell'*
These verses could be sung by dead soldiers replying to Edwin
Lutyens, one of the main war cemetery architects. He was

visiting the Ypres battle sites when he wrote this description in a letter home: 'a ribbon of isolated graves like a milky way across miles of country where men were tucked in where they fell.'

5 *'Their Name Liveth For Evermore'*

This wording appeared on many war memorials. How to name and record the dead of 1914–1918 was a strikingly prominent question. The ideal of dignifying those lost beyond any hope of burial produced the emblematic figure of the Unknown Soldier. 'Their Name Liveth For Evermore' was engraved on many war memorials including the Menin Gate at Ypres. This monument invoked another, would-be consoling, rubric; 'He is not missing; he is here.' My speakers offer their own laconic thoughts on this matter of names without bodies, bodies without names.

6 *'Death of a Hero'*

A note on post-war aesthetic isolation, as if by some 'modernist' writer: *Death of a Hero* is the title of Richard Aldington's 1929 novel about the unhappy return of a disenchanted soldier.

7 *'He lies somewhere in France'. Somewhere.*

The phrase 'He lies somewhere in France' often indicated an untraceable body. What do you do when you have no body to bury, and you're also well aware that your own loss is the tiniest part of a global catastrophe? Arthur Conan Doyle wrote 'All that I can do is be a gramophone on the subject', referring to his spiritualist conviction of the reality of contact with the war dead. The line 'I fought for strength and tearlessness and found both' is from a diary entry by Alda, Lady Hoare, made during her son's last leave before he was killed. It's in her manuscript 'This Short Sketch of the Life of Our Son', 1916.

Acknowledgements

I'm enormously grateful to all those editors who, whether from the 1970s or onward into this century, have resolutely extracted and encouraged the work represented in this selection – prominent among whom are Wendy Mulford, Ken Edwards, and Don Paterson. Thank you, too, to Kishani Widyaratna for her editing skills in assembling this book.